THE PROFESSIONAL COMMODITY TRADER

By the same author

The Commodity Futures Market Guide
    (*with Irwin Shishko*)

THE PROFESSIONAL COMMODITY TRADER

(LOOK OVER MY SHOULDER)

STANLEY KROLL

HARPER & ROW, PUBLISHERS

NEW YORK

EVANSTON

SAN FRANCISCO

LONDON

1817

Designed by Sidney Feinberg

Library of Congress Cataloging in Publication Data

Kroll, Stanley.
   The professional commodity trader (look over my shoulder)
   1. Commodity exchanges—United States.   2. Speculation.   I. Title.
HG6046.K82   332.6'44   74–1827
ISBN 0–06–012468–7

To Jarrett,
wife, companion, editor, and helmsman
and to my three daughters
and mini-enthusiasts,
Laura, Beverly, and Janet

*The surest way to make
a small fortune in the
commodity market is to
start with a large one*

Contents

Preface

Since the early 1970s, commodity trading has received more attention than ever before from investors and observers alike. Small wonder, then, that more and more people would like to delve into the mind of the successful professional trader to discover how he operates, what makes him tick, and what are the secrets, if any, of his success.

Well, we tick like most other folks—although sometimes our "tickers" accelerate in direct proportion to the upswings or downturns in the market.

The secret of success: knowledge of the markets and of particular commodities, an understanding of both the fundamental and technical aspects of each market, fast reflexes and a good sense of timing, a bit of luck, and a great deal of patience and courage. Add lots of experience, a few "burns," and a goodly number of "killings," and you're on your way.

Clearly, big money can be made in commodity trading. But the profits seem more elusive than real, for nearly all speculators —including many professionals—end up losers, many in a big way. Of course, for every dollar lost by the majority of traders, a happy few profit by the same amount.

This book is, if you will, something of a jaunt through the (business) life style of a rapidly increasing number of people worldwide. It is estimated that there are some 500,000 active commodity traders in the United States alone, and countless others throughout the financial centers of the world. And they are trading more actively each year, as can be seen from Figure 1.

Here is an intimate guided tour inside the exciting, fast-moving world of the professional commodity trader. Look over his

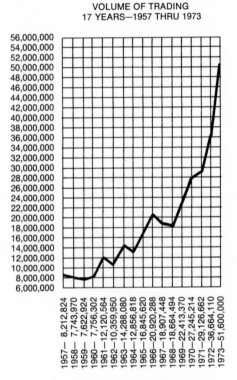

VOLUME OF TRADING
17 YEARS—1957 THRU 1973

1957— 8,212,824
1958— 7,743,970
1959— 7,622,924
1960— 7,756,302
1961—12,120,564
1962—10,359,950
1963—14,288,080
1964—12,856,818
1965—16,845,620
1966—20,920,288
1967—18,907,448
1968—18,664,494
1969—22,413,370
1970—27,245,214
1971—29,126,662
1972—36,664,110
1973—51,600,000

Figure 1.   Chart courtesy of the Association
of Commodity Exchange Firms, Inc.

shoulder as he operates in a market where fortunes can be made or lost overnight—where one can buy or sell $140,000 worth of a commodity future for just $4,000 margin, or 2.9 percent of the total market value.

This book brings you firsthand into the meetings and conferences, the transatlantic Telex and telephone conversations—the very private maneuvers of the professional market operator. What general and specific rules and guidelines does he use? What about econometric studies and market advisory letters? How you can let profits run but cut losses short—how to *actually* do it, not just talk about doing it. Learn how to avoid overtrading, yet still be there with a substantial position when they divvy the profits at the end of a major move.

Mistakes, miscalculations, errors of judgment—and there are plenty of them—are candidly discussed, analyzed, and critiqued. The successful professional is more concerned with analyzing his bad trades than with crowing about his good ones.

Some of my associates suggested that I write an exposé-type book about the commodity business—they seem to be quite popular now. I did read several of the Wall Street exposé books and found them generally entertaining but not very helpful in trading. I was even advised by some to make it sexy and exciting—two prime ingredients for a successful Wall Street book.

Well, this is an exposé book—of sorts. I hope to expose how to trade successfully and profitably; to lose less on your losing trades and to gain more on profitable ones.

And if sex and excitement will sell a book, this may very well be a best seller. Have you ever been long 100,000 bushels of soybeans, or twenty silver contracts (200,000 troy ounces), with the market moving up sharply—and maybe hitting a few consecutive limit moves, too? Sexy and exciting? Well, everything is relative.

Any book which claims to deal with the intricacies of a specialized financial market must assume that its readers will have some familiarity with the subject at hand. At the very least, the reader should be comfortable with the common terminology which applies to most financial markets.

If you are experienced with trading—either stocks or bonds, or in day-to-day business dealings—then you can probably swing into this book rather easily. If, however, you are just considering taking the plunge, read the quick what-it's-all-about appendix for your orientation. When you are ready to delve further into the subject, you ought to get a copy of my earlier book.*

I remember, as a youngster, being given a booklet about how to improve one's baseball batting average. Imagine my disappointment when, upon reading the introduction, I was unable to

---

* *The Commodity Futures Market Guide,* by Stanley Kroll and Irwin Shishko (Harper & Row, 1973).

SUMMARY OF MANAGED ACCOUNTS
For the Period July 1971 Through January 1974

Starting Date	Client	Capital Invested	Current Equity 1-11-74	Cash Withdrawn	Total Equity	Increase (Decrease)	Percentage (Annualized)
07-11-71	CMS	$ 18,000	$ 730,789	—	$ 730,789	$ 712,789	1,634
11-22-71	# 1	17,460	87,444	40,445	127,889	110,429	292
11-22-71	# 2	10,000	—	72,176	72,176	62,176	310
11-30-71	# 3	51,000	77,934	42,000	119,934	68,934	62
12-01-71	# 4	11,990	57,561	11,988	69,549	57,559	221
12-01-71	# 5	5,000	—	17,155	17,155	12,155	153
12-09-71	# 6	35,000	—	93,604	93,604	58,604	105
12-20-72	# 7	25,000	22,770	47,538	70,308	45,308	84
01-21-72	# 8	16,735	—	93,080	93,080	76,345	304
04-05-72	# 9	5,000	—	13,635	13,635	8,635	187
04-12-72	#10	21,000	18,677	20,432	39,109	18,109	49
04-12-72	#11	2,565	90,693	22,500	113,191	110,626	2,474
05-03-72	#12	7,500	—	21,265	21,265	13,765	366
05-18-72	#13	25,000	—	46,400	46,400	21,400	102
08-16-72	#14	20,000	—	24,908	24,908	4,908	72
08-23-72	#15	17,832	—	21,844	21,844	4,012	20
09-13-72	#16	20,000	—	38,914	38,914	18,914	225
09-13-72	#17	15,000	137,312	4,900	142,212	127,212	630
10-18-72	#18	19,297	48,285	18,700	66,985	47,688	197
11-01-72	#19	30,000	91,185	22,700	113,885	83,885	239

Date	#						
11-01-72	#20	15,000	—	43,389	43,389	28,389	567
11-01-72	#21	20,000	—	91,477	91,477	71,477	428
12-03-72	#22	10,000	71,307	24,500	95,807	85,807	792
12-23-72	#23	10,500	33,283	13,000	46,283	35,783	314
01-14-73	#24	10,000	6,060	12,000	18,060	8,060	76
01-24-73	#25	6,000	5,636	13,900	19,536	13,536	213
02-23-73	#26	10,000	—	9,839	9,839	(161)	(1.6)
02-23-73	#27	25,000	111,611	17,000	128,611	103,611	448
03-02-73	#28	10,000	—	20,302	20,302	10,302	206
03-02-73	#29	7,500	5,921	19,000	24,921	17,421	277
03-15-73	#30	30,000	147,933	—	147,933	117,933	479
04-10-73	#31	5,000	24,223	4,500	28,723	23,723	629
05-03-73	#32	30,000	60,465	—	60,465	30,465	152
05-16-73	#33	15,000	7,744	12,896	20,640	5,640	56
05-17-73	#34	10,000	19,498	—	19,498	9,498	141
05-18-73	#35	40,000	71,453	—	71,453	71,453	117
06-20-73	#36	22,000	56,186	—	56,186	34,186	265
06-20-73	#37	5,000	—	5,394	5,394	394	19
09-10-73	#38	10,000	—	39,787	39,787	29,787	891
TOTALS:		$664,379	$1,983,970	$1,001,168	$2,985,138	$2,320,759	

find the author's personal batting average. Even at that tender age, it seemed to me, a writer of a baseball batting book should declare his batting average at the outset. I had never heard of the author and, for all I knew, he had never even held a bat in his hands, not to mention knowing the fine points of wielding one.

Well, I still feel the same way, and it's some thirty years later. People should know your "batting average" before they take your "how to bat" book seriously. Since this is my "how to trade" book, I'll save you the trouble of scanning for my trading record. Here it is.

It covers the period July 1971 through January 1974—a most volatile and difficult 2½-year period for Wall Street. And it summarizes the trading results of the 39 accounts I've managed—one of them, Commodity Management Services (CMS), being my own —on a discretionary basis.

The bottom line says that I've turned $664,379 into $2,985,138 since July 1971, of which $1,001,168 has been taken out in cash.

What it doesn't show are the headaches, heartaches, and stomachaches, the frustration, agitation, and uncertainty, the exultation and triumph as well as the dismal defeats, of those past years. But those I'll tell you about in the following pages.

What Do You Do for an Encore?

1

What do you do for an encore after you've just turned $350,000 into $900,000 in the commodity game in a year and a half? You promptly drop a quick $150,000 on the short side of wheat and sugar, that's what. Some encore!

Then you spend the next few days brooding and kicking yourself in the ass . . . bitching at your wife, overeating and under-sleeping.

A  conversation:

"Everything is moving the wrong way. I mean, every market we're in is just going against us . . . it's unbelievable. What am I doing about it? I'm perspiring plenty and aggravating myself, that's what I'm doing about it.

"Sugar is up 18 points and suddenly everyone who was bearish last week while it was going down is getting bullish. Every time sugar moves up, Brazil is 'about to' raise its selling prices; every time the market sells off, Brazil is 'about to' lower its prices. The speculators get jerked around every time.

"I think sugar is a great short; on the other hand, I'm the only one

1

who thinks so. The 'specs' won't get bearish until it's already down a few hundred points.

"Remember the long cotton position we sold out last week with good profits? New highs again today. No, I'm not short—big deal—but it's up already 50 points from where we sold out. What timing! And copper—my budding bull market—new lows for the week.

"Well, let's see, what else is going wrong? Oh yes, our long silver position is only down 200 points today, and wheat is strong—up about two cents. Of course I'm short wheat, what do you think?

"That's the way it goes. At least we have plenty of margin money, so I'm not *forced* to liquidate anything—unless I want to. Matter of fact, I sold a little more wheat on a rally this morning, but I'm not too crazy about that position—think I'll cover it in a little while. And copper . . . if it makes new lows again this afternoon, I'll buy more. . . . I'll keep on buying more copper. It's going much higher.

"We just have to sit through times like these; sometimes we just have to take our medicine. We have good times and bad, and this is one of the bad . . . but 'sitting' is where we'll make the big money . . . the big money."

Meanwhile, the managed-account clients gradually wake up to the fact that they're short those two unmentionable commodities—and that both markets are going up (not down, as they're supposed to). And they all start calling. People who used to call once a month start calling every few days. And what do they talk about? They ask how I'm feeling, and what's new? How's silver and soybeans? (They never mention the unmentionable short positions.) And they even discuss—would you believe it?—politics, sports, and the weather. The weather?

After a few days of self-doubt and manic-depressive feelings, you do what must be done. You close out the "unmentionable" positions and take the big losses; then you go back to the drawing board. Which in this case consists of the charts, statistical data, a clear head, and an optimistic, confident attitude; also an objective critique of what you did right and wrong in the market.

An Objective Critique . . .

2

A. . . . . *Of What We Did Right*

A critical review of a profitable trading period, during which we more than doubled our trading capital in the seven months from November 1971 through May 1972, reveals some interesting patterns.

Our most profitable and successful trading campaign was in silver. It was successful because:

1. We were quick to perceive the newly developing upward market trend in November and December of 1971, and essentially we maintained long positions (following the prevailing trend) during most of this period.

2. We traded with the major (up) trend *and* against the minor trend, buying on minor downtrends—such as the 10¢ reaction in December 1971, the 7¢ reaction in January 1972, and the extended 12¢ dip in February—when the majority of speculators had assumed a bearish posture and were selling. Moreover, we followed a policy of selling out a part of our long position whenever (a) the market had attained our upside trading objective, *and* (b) the minor trend had turned up, *and* (c) prices were "digging" into formidable overhead resistance. Invariably, the prevailing market sentiment was most bullish during those rallies.

3. We *absolutely* resisted all temptations (and there were many) to trade with the prevailing mass sentiment; that is, to buy on rallies and to sell on declines. (Figure 2.)

Another successful trade was our cocoa campaign of December

Commodity Chart Service, Commodity Research Bureau Inc.

Figure 2.

1971 through February 1972, which culminated in our sale of a sizable block of May futures around the 25.30 level on the morning of February 8, 1972. As a matter of fact, the venerable Commodity News Service "broad tape" flashed its subscribers on that morning that a large trade house had stopped the market by selling a large quantity of cocoa on the opening. (It was just us, folks!)

As with silver, we made money because we correctly gauged the intermediate-to-major (upward) trend of the market following the triple bottom at the 21.00 level in November and December of 1971. We kept buying, but only on reactions into support. The position was finally sold on February 8 because:

1. The market had attained our intermediate price objective.

2. Prevailing market sentiment had turned overwhelmingly bullish and the minor trend had just turned up (remember, we try to trade *with* the major trend and *against* the minor trend).

3. Prices were bumping into major overhead resistance around the 26.00 level, and we felt that a substantial price correction would likely precede any further advance.

An interesting sidelight to this cocoa campaign: our initial purchase of May cocoa was made on December 21, around 21.40. At that time, we projected that the market could decline temporarily to 20.50 without disturbing our bullish prognosis; and if it did react to that level, we would "double up" on our long May position. The market did in fact decline to 20.40 on December 30, but we didn't buy more—we very unprofessionally chickened out, having succumbed to the speculator's universal malaise of becoming bearish on price declines. We should have stuck to our original strategy, and we resolved to do so in the future. (Figure 3.)

Our three notable break-even trades during this period were in cattle, cotton, and copper. We were short cattle and cotton, having sold both against a minor uptrend into overhead resistance. Both markets ultimately turned into full-fledged bull markets, stopping out our short positions at no-loss stop orders. The reason that we didn't lose money on these trades—and by all odds we should have lost money, being short in what proved to be bull markets—was that our shorts were initiated on minor rallies into overhead resistance. Had we instead sold on the downturns, when the majority of speculators were turning bearish and when conventional chart analysis had mandated selling, our losses would have been substantial.

I almost break out in a cold sweat when I think of our copper

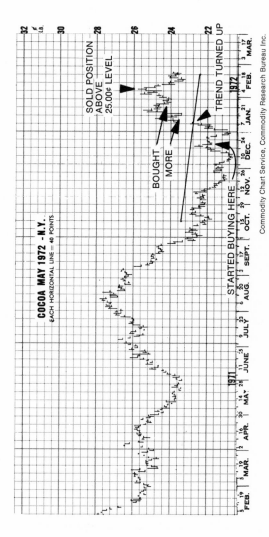

Figure 3.

Commodity Chart Service, Commodity Research Bureau Inc.

campaign of early 1972. It was a tremendously volatile market and we experienced successively early exultation, smashing surprise (no, horror!), and, finally, record relief. Here's how it happened:

Early exultation. The copper market, in January 1972, looked like a good buy. The recent November break, down to the 46.00 level, basis May, appeared to be the culmination of an extended two-year bear market that had carried prices down from 77.00¢ to 45.00¢ a pound. Prices had substantially exceeded all major downside "count"* objectives, and the market was getting strong and broad buying support on all reactions. Moreover, the 46.00 level coincided with the top of a supersolid, long-term support area.

Following an uncorrected advance from the 46.00 bottom to 50.00 and the subsequent 50 percent retracement back down to 48.00, we accumulated a long position of about 150 contracts. We were anticipating much higher prices, and when the market rallied to 51.60 we weren't much surprised. So preoccupied were we with counting our forthcoming profits that we failed to spot a potential reversal building up at the 51.50 level, until it happened.

Smashing surprise horror. Have you ever considered what it might be like to sit long 150 copper contracts through two down-limit days? Well, you could buy five Rolls-Royces with your losings or 1.5 million 10¢ candy bars, presuming you could get them at 10¢. In short, we had just watched some $150,000 change hands (the wrong direction) in just 48 hours. How's *that* for a horror story?

Record relief. We sat (extremely) tight after the great bull massacre, which carried prices down to 47.70 for May, waiting for a rally to close out our position. The market collapse had apparently shaken out enough weak longs to strengthen the technical condition of the market. Four or five days later, when the market rallied back to 50.00, we dumped our entire 150 contracts. A potential first-class disaster was averted, and we ultimately closed out at a small profit because we:

a. Purchased our initial long position on reactions into support, against the minor downtrend.

---

* Price objective based on technical (chart) analysis.

b. Held tight while the market was getting killed.

c. Closed out the entire long position on the subsequent 50 percent retracement rally into overhead resistance. (Figure 4.)

At one time or another, every trader has wished for a copy of tomorrow's prices. Unfortunately, such opportunities occur only in the imagination. Perhaps almost as valuable is the opportunity to examine a detailed record of one's thoughts and market action for a past campaign, in the light of how the situation actually developed. Let's start by looking back some 10 months, to February 1972, when I wrote the following notes on our forthcoming soybean campaign:

> In soybeans, I see a promising bull market potential. Our first long position was initiated on January 12, 1972, at 3.17 for May, on a reaction down to the 3.14 to 3.18 support area. We subsequently bought more Mays around 3.19, more at 3.21, and more at 3.24. This last purchase, in particular, wasn't warranted. We were (prematurely) anticipating a close above 3.25–3.26, which would have been bullish (but which didn't occur), and we were buying with the minor (up) trend and with the public (neither of which we fancy doing).
>
> We took partial profits between 3.22 and 3.24 and rebought (even more this time) on the succeeding decline to the 3.20 level. This was fine, as we shouldn't be reluctant to take partial profits on rallies into overhead resistance when the major trend is still sideways to down. Our subsequent sale of one-quarter our long position, on a stop-loss at 3.18⅜, was a protective maneuver which probably wouldn't have been mandated had we not bought that batch of Mays at 3.24.
>
> Now we are projecting higher soybean prices. Our basic market approach will be to maintain long positions, to trade with the major (up) trend against the minor countertrends. More specifically, we will wait for the major trend to turn up (which we expect will happen shortly) and then add to our long position *only* on minor reactions. We will eventually have a substantial long position, but only if the major trend is up and our early positions are held at profits.

Well, that's what I wrote about the soybean market back in February 1972. In December, some ten months later, let's see what actually happened.

We were holding a substantial long position of May beans when the market turned strongly upward (with a close above 3.26). When, during the week of February 28, we liquidated our entire line between 3.34 and 3.36, we were pleased because:

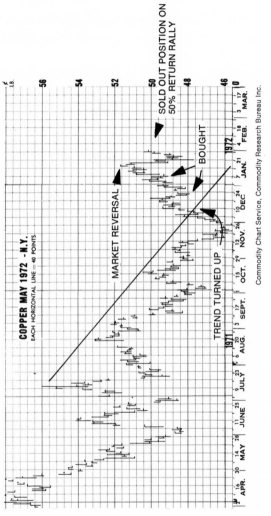

Figure 4.

Commodity Chart Service, Commodity Research Bureau Inc.

1. We had more than doubled our money in two months.

2. The market had attained our intermediate price objective of 3.35 and was coming into major overhead resistance between 3.35 and 3.40.

3. We projected a reaction to at least the 3.30 level, where we would rebuy an even bigger long position than the one we had recently sold out.

Following our sale, the bean market kept going up, up, up, and away—to the incredible, unbelievable price of 4.40, in just ten months. And while we had, in fact, taken a 15¢ profit, we watched incredulously *as the market advanced an additional 105¢ per bushel.**

The lesson to be learned here is this: if you want to make really big money in commodity trading (and that's the only reason to be trading), don't scalp for quick, small trades no matter how enticing they may appear. You should premise that each of your important market positions will continue for a major move and plan your strategy accordingly. Certainly, you've got to be quick to close out if the major trend turns against you, but don't be in any rush to close out while the market is still moving favorably. Remember, *the major trend invariably runs longer and further than you expect it to.* (Figure 5.)

B. . . . *And Of What We Did Wrong*

We went short sugar and wheat in the midst of the Great Bull Market of 1972—that's what we did wrong! Having missed the long side of these two markets (and that's really inexcusable), we got suckered into the novice trader's classic bonehead play: we got prematurely bearish. And what happens when you're prematurely bearish? (in a bull market, of course). You go prematurely short. The outcome is predictable; you get prematurely gray and unexpectedly poor. Here's what happened:

Sugar is sweeter. Starting from a base of 5.00¢ in November of 1971, March 1973 sugar bulled its way up to the 9.00¢ level by early March 1972. There is an old Wall Street adage: "Every bull market sows the seeds of its ultimate bear-market reversal," and

---

* A \$4.40 soybean price turned out not to be so incredible and unbelievable, after all. By June 1973, soybeans had advanced to \$12.90 per bushel.

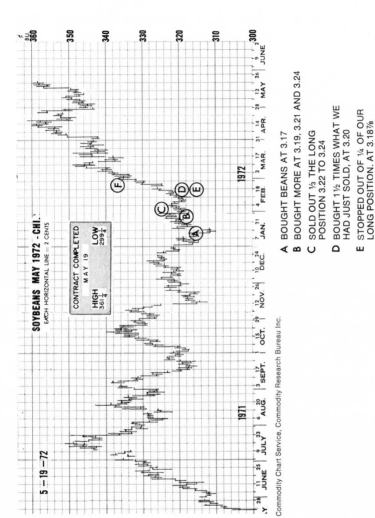

SOYBEANS MAY 1972 - CHI.
EACH HORIZONTAL LINE = 2 CENTS

CONTRACT COMPLETED
MAY 19

HIGH
361¼

LOW
299¼

5 — 19 —72

1971

1972

Commodity Chart Service, Commodity Research Bureau Inc.

A   BOUGHT BEANS AT 3.17

B   BOUGHT MORE AT 3.19, 3.21 AND 3.24

C   SOLD OUT ⅓ THE LONG
    POSITION 3.22 TO 3.24

D   BOUGHT 1½ TIMES WHAT WE
    HAD JUST SOLD, AT 3.20

E   STOPPED OUT OF ¼ OF OUR
    LONG POSITION, AT 3.18⅞

F   LIQUIDATED ENTIRE LONG
    POSITION BETWEEN 3.34 AND 3.36

Figure 5.

this sugar market was no exception. From the March rally high the market eroded, over a 4-month period, back to the 5.50¢ level. Quite a roller coaster, this one, as prices then rallied from 5.50¢ to 8.50¢ between the beginning of August 1972 and the first week of September. A massive sidewise trading range then developed, in the shape of a large symmetrical triangle, with ascending bottoms at points A, B, and C (see Figure 6) and descending tops at points D, E, and F.

It was this large sideways triangle formation which we interpreted as a potential top with a definite bearish bias. We shorted a good quantity of Marches around 7.70¢ in mid-October, and covered half the position under 7.20¢ on the subsequent reaction to the 7.00¢ support level. On the next return rally to 7.80¢ we resold the shorts we had recently covered. So far so good, *but not for long.* Prices then advanced through the 7.80¢ resistance level, and that should have tipped us off that (maybe) this was still a bull market. On December 1 the market moved decisively up through 8.15¢, a clear upside breakout from the massive three-month triangle formation (there we were, still short our position from 7.70¢), and it closed with a resounding 8.24¢.

There was no doubt now that we were wrong—we were short a large position in a strong bull trend—and we should have had the foresight to cover our entire line at the close that day.

Well, hope springs eternal in the heart of the trapped commodity trader. Our decision (which we are still regretting) was not to cover on the close at 8.24¢ but to wait for the next reaction, to around the 7.80¢ level, and cover there.

The rest is history; the market kept advancing, right on up to the 10.12¢ level, before encountering any significant resistance. In the process, we lost both our short position and nearly $70,000 of our trading capital.

Dickson G. Watts, the famous nineteenth-century cotton trader, once said, "Run quickly, or not at all." We should have run quickly:

—when the market surpassed the 7.80¢ previous high and the downtrend line. This was the first "danger signal," and we should have covered at least half (if not all) of the position there;

—and on December 1, when prices exploded through 8.15¢ and closed at 8.24¢. Any remaining shorts should have been covered on that close. (Figure 6.)

We got all wet in wheat. Just to prove that our disaster in the Great Sugar Market was no mere accident, we pulled the same imbecilic stunt in the second-greatest wheat bull market in history.

The Chicago wheat market had advanced from $1.50 in late June 1972 to $2.32 by mid-September. What a fantastic move it was! Enormous volume, the open-interest doubling, and finally, lots of publicity about Chinese and Soviet wheat purchases. At that point the market declined to the $2.10 level, rallied back into the top area at $2.27, and then reacted down to $2.17. I viewed the market as making a major top and decided to go short on the next rally, because:

1. The advance to $2.32 exceeded my most bullish upside price projection and coincided with a major long-term overhead resistance level.

2. It appeared that all the news which had fueled the bull move, i.e., large-scale Chinese and Soviet wheat purchases, was already known and hence was discounted in the market price.

3. The public was overwhelmingly (78 percent) bullish* and the open interest had advanced from 50 million bushels at the beginning of the move to 100 million bushels. I deemed this to indicate an extremely vulnerable market.

4. The recent sideways price action appeared to be a distribution area at the top, and I viewed rallies in this area as excellent short sales.

So, I let out about 400,000 bushels of Marches around $2.23 to $2.24.

Talk about timing! On the next day wheat began a "modest" 6-week rally, which carried prices straight up to $2.73¼.

Actually, I had two perfect opportunities to cover the shorts at a small loss: when the market closed at $2.33½ on November 15 (new life-of-contract highs) and again on the subsequent reaction to $2.28¼ on November 21. An interesting sidelight: I had determined to cover on any decline below $2.30, but when prices

---

* According to *Market Vane,* Pasadena, California.

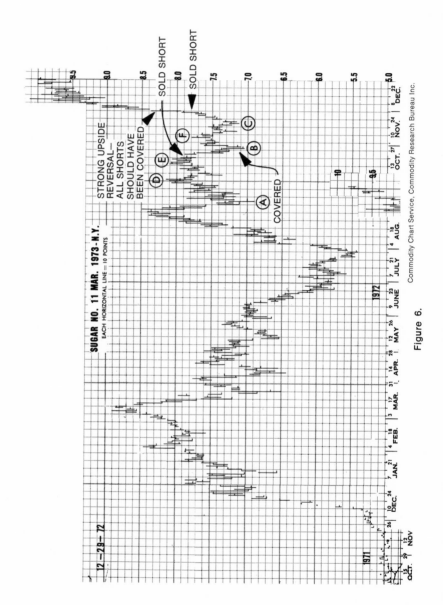

SUGAR NO. 11 MAR. 1973-N.Y.
EACH HORIZONTAL LINE = 10 POINTS

STRONG UPSIDE REVERSAL— ALL SHORTS SHOULD HAVE BEEN COVERED

SOLD SHORT

SOLD SHORT

COVERED

Figure 6.

Commodity Chart Service, Commodity Research Bureau Inc.

12-29-72

WHEAT MAR. 1973 - CHI.
EACH HORIZONTAL LINE = 2 CENTS

COVERED SHORTS

SHOULD HAVE COVERED SHORTS

SOLD SHORT

1972   1973

TOTAL OPEN INTEREST &
VOLUME (All Contracts)

OPEN INTEREST
(1966-1971 AVG.)

CURRENT OPEN INTEREST

VOLUME

14 28 12 26 9 23 7 21 4 18 1 15 29 13 27 10 24 8 22 5 19 2 1
APR. | MAY | JUNE | JULY | AUG. | SEPT. | OCT. | NOV. | DEC. | JAN. | FE

Commodity Chart Service, Commodity Research Bureau Inc.

Figure 7.

actually got down to $2.28½ I became greedy and opted for an additional 2¢ decline. I never got it.

What a dumb play! I eventually covered part of the position around $2.44 and more at $2.54, all the while hoping vainly for any kind of reaction to cover the balance. The last 60,000 bushels were covered at $2.70 (ouch!), spilling lots of red ink along the way.

What is it we're always saying about *cutting losses* and letting profits run? (Figure 7.)

It's a Living

3

An interview with Q, a free-lance financial writer:

Q: There seems to be the perennial problem of whether one should use fundamental or technical analysis in analyzing commodity markets. Are you a fundamentalist or a technician?

SK: Well, I do study the fundamentals, plus the news developments and the various economic reports, and I'm constantly talking with people in the trade, but really, I just don't have a workable handle on trading the markets using just fundamentals.

Q: I often wonder how many people do trade solely on fundamental considerations. And how do they do in the market?

SK: I have yet to see anyone trade just on fundamentals and make money. Sometimes they say they're using only fundamentals, but if you watch them operate, you'll find they are watching the price action too—in effect, keeping "mental" charts. I think the astute and patient technician will generally outperform the fundamental trader, because his timing is bound to be more accurate. He can trade more flexibly, be in and out a lot faster when it counts, and will probably

17

take smaller, more accurate positions. The risk is that the chartist may try to pinpoint the moves so closely that he'll never have a meaningful position for a major move—that's what he has to guard against.

11:10 A.M. (on the phone to the Chicago broker): "Let's buy 15 April cattle contracts at the market—and also buy 15 June cattle at the market. Yes, that's right, I'm buying 30 cattle at the market."

Q: Why did you do that? Why did you just buy cattle? We were just sitting and talking, so what made you decide to buy?

SK: I'm buying cattle for a combination of reasons. First, I've been generally bullish on cattle for the past few days, and am trying to accumulate gradually a fair-size long position.

Second, the market's been down over 300 points during recent sessions, and it's coming into a good support level, around 47.00. I can see it down from here, perhaps another 100 points—and I'll be a buyer there—but beyond that, I'm looking for higher prices.

Finally, corn and beans, which had been weak recently, are starting to rally. Cattle prices depend on feed prices to a great extent, and I don't see any near-term weakness in feeds—so I think cattle prices will move up with the grains.

Q: Well, that sounds clear enough. Hope you're right. But look, we're just sitting here talking, and you seem so calm and relaxed, and this entire office is so quiet. I've never seen a brokerage office like this. You are very busy—I know that. How and why do you manage to maintain everything so low-key?

SK: Well, I operate this way for one simple reason: I work most efficiently like this. My mind is clear, I'm not distracted, and I can concentrate fully. And this kind of work requires the utmost concentration.

Q: O.K., but exactly how do you operate? Could you summarize that for me?

SK: Yes, I think so. My operation is basically very simple—surprisingly uncomplicated. Essentially, when I arrive at my office at 9:15 in the morning, most of my day's work is already completed.

Q: I'm willing to take your word for it that it's simple, but it can't be that simple.

SK: Well, not quite. Most of my work is done after the close of the market, each day. Starting around three o'clock, I post my charts, call around to the floors and some of the trade houses, reread the day's cables and news tapes, and generally formulate my ideas on the various markets.

After all this, I concentrate on a special form which I designed a couple of years ago.*

Filling out this form imposes a kind of discipline on my analysis—it effectively forces me to identify, objectively and rationally, all the significant technical factors for each commodity:

1. Trend (major and minor).
2. Support area (major and minor).
3. Resistance area (major and minor).
4. Trading range or trend channel.
5. Price objective (major and minor).
6. General comments or things to look out for.

Then I take action.

Q: May I see the form that you're currently using? Oh, I see how it looks. But aren't you concerned that if it's such a good method, if many others start using it, they'll ruin the system for you?

SK: Not at all. First, it's not a "system." It's just an extremely useful tool—successful trading still depends on someone making a precise and final determination of what to buy or sell, and *where* to do it. Furthermore, I doubt whether anyone will even try using this approach. Commodity traders, as a group, are an egotistical bunch, and each one figures that his particular method is the only one that's any good.

Q: That's interesting. But it certainly doesn't seem to make logical sense.

SK: That's for sure.

* See Figure 8.

AS OF FRI 12/28/73

COMMODITY	TREND		SUPPORT		RESISTANCE		TRADING RANGE TREND CHANNEL		PRICE OBJ.		COMMENT	TAKE ACTION
	MAJOR	MINOR	MAJOR	MINOR	MAJOR	MINOR	TOP	BOTTOM	MAJOR	MINOR		
COCOA - MAY	↑	←	4500	5100	6100-6300	5450-5550	60.00	50.00	70.00	60.00	VERY BULLISH ACTION	BUY 5000-5200
PLATINUM											MARKET IS TOO THIN & VOLATILE	STAND ASIDE
SILVER - MAY	←	←	2.80-2.90	3.60	5.50-6.00	3.40-3.60	?	?	5.60	3.60	VERY BULLISH ACTION	HOLD LONGS SELL 1/2 @ 3.50 HOLD BALANCE
SUGAR - MAY	←	←	10.00-10.50	11.50	18.00	12.50	?	?	18.00	13.00	VERY BULLISH TOO RISKY	STAND ASIDE - BUY ON REACTION TO 10.50
COPPER - SEPT.	←	←	70.00	7500	95.00-100.00	80.00	8000	7500	9500-100.00	80.00 to 8500	MKT IS INVERTED SO WE ARE BUYING FUTURES AT DISCOUNT	BUY AT CURRENT LEVEL (7500) AND MORE ON CLOSE OVER 8000 HOLD LONGS WITH 40 STOPS
CATTLE (CME) APRIL	↑	←	4500-4600	46.00	5500-5700	53.00	5000	4000	5600-5800	53.00	CLOSE OVER 50.00 IS BULLISH	HOLD LONGS- BUY MORE ON CLOSE OVER 50.00 SELL @ 55.00
CORN - MAY	←	↑	250	270	300-310	280	280	270	300-310	285	CLOSE OVER 280 IS BULLISH	HOLD LONGS- BUY MORE ON CLOSE OVER 280 SELL 1/2 POSITION 300-310
- MAY PORK BELLIES	→	→	4600-5000	60.00	7000-7200	6400-6500	6600	5900	4700	5500	CLOSE OVER 6100 IS BULLISH	SELL SHORT 6500-WITH STOP-LOSS PROTECTION 6700 CLOSE-ONLY COVER 1/2 5700
POTATOES											MARKET TOO VOLATILE	STAND ASIDE
SOYBEANS - MAY	↑	↑	540-560	540-600	750-800	650	650	580	750-800	650	CLOSE OVER 650 IS BULLISH	BUY AT CURRENT LEVEL (625) AND MORE ON CLOSE OVER 650. PROTECT WITH 20¢ STOP-LOSS
WHEAT											LOOKS BULLISH BUT SEEMS TOO RISKY TO TRADE	STAND ASIDE

Figure 8.

Q: Look, I think we're on to something here, and I don't want to drop it. O.K., it's late afternoon, you've posted your charts, made your phone calls, and you've finished posting your trading sheet. What next?

SK: Well, by now I have some general ideas on what I'm interested in buying or selling—or, in the case of existing market positions, how I generally feel about them. I now focus intently on each of the markets I've been tracking. It's amazing how clearly and objectively you can analyze a market when the board is shut down, the tickers are quiet, and the phones aren't ringing. I prefer to hold positions that are in the direction of the major trend—and, if I'm thinking about adding to a position, I'd like to add *against* the minor trend.

Q: Could you be a little more specific on that point? How about giving me an actual example?

SK: I figured you'd ask that one. O.K. Silver has been in a broad, major uptrend since December of 1971, and I've been long the market much of the time. Sure, we've had our wild price swings, both up and down, but the big money in silver has been made on the long side; that is, the traders who ignored the short-term swings and concentrated on holding positions in the direction of the major trend—they made the really big money.

But identifying the major trend is only half the job, because the swings are so broad that you could get killed even being long if you bought at the wrong time. So during the past year or two, I've concentrated on being long the market and adding to positions on minor reactions—in effect, when the minor trend turned down. My rationale was this: the major trend is up, and it's going to stay up for some time; therefore, buy on weakness and count on the major uptrend to reassert itself after each weak spell.

Q: You've certainly answered my question. But let's get back to our basic discussion. You were talking about using your trading card to help in making the buy and sell decisions.

SK: Yes. If I consider buying, is the major trend up and the minor trend down? If so, where should the market find good support? I scale "limit" buying orders at that point (limit orders specify the price I'm bidding for the contracts). If I'm interested in buying and the major trend is down, then I've got to have pretty strong reasons, based on other solid technical considerations, for doing so. In most cases, I end up staying away from those situations. There are enough markets where I can find trends that really suit me, so why get involved where I start with one or two strikes against me at the outset?

Q: What about getting out of positions? I see all kinds of little notations on your charts, such as "Sell here" or "Good support, start buying."

SK: On the basis of rather conventional technical analysis—please don't ask me to detail what I mean by that, we could be here all night, and you'll have to read *The Commodity Futures Market Guide* because it's all in there—I formulate and project price objectives; both short-term and long-term. If the trend isn't too solid, I'll start scaling out some stuff when the market attains my short-term objective. However, if the trend looks strong and is supported by other technical indicators—such as open interest and volume—then I'll probably hold off liquidating and wait for my major price objective to be reached. That will usually coincide with a solid support area in the case of a major downtrend, or a significant overhead resistance area in an uptrend. There's a great tendency to get carried away with the prevailing market psychology at that time and not do any liquidating. But you've got to resist that tendency; when the market attains your major price objective, where you had projected closing out, say, half the position, *do it!* If you don't, you'll probably regret it later. You may want to keep half the positions open, on the assumption that no one ever picks the top or bottom of a move and you'll have a better spot later. O.K., but at least close out half the position there.

Q: What happens when something catches your attention during a trading session, something that you may not have noted on your trading card the previous evening?

SK: Certainly, if something happens unexpectedly—and that is a frequent occurrence—I do react to it. It may be sudden action of the prices, it may be a news item on the Reuters ticker, or even a phone call offering a tip or some pit gossip.

Q: A tip? Do you mean to say that you get tips in the market? What do you do when you get a tip?

SK: Sure, I get tips all the time. Mostly from my clients, who heard something on the train or at a cocktail party. Well, I'll admit that if it sounds like even a reasonably good idea, I'll check it out. Sometimes it puts me on to something I may have overlooked.

Q: Hmmm. How about an example?

SK: About six weeks ago, I'm sitting and watching the board when RH calls and says I should look at soybeans. He hears talk of heavy bean demand for both export and crush, which should be bullish.

Q: Well, what did you do? Did you follow the tip?

SK: I had been tracking beans already, and was looking for a spot to start buying. Perhaps RH's call triggered the "buy button," but I did start buying there.

Q: How did this particular tip work out?

SK: Pretty well, although I did have to sweat the position for another three weeks. The so-called tip came when May beans were trading around 5.60; the market subsequently traded as low as 5.20 and as high as 6.50. So I'll never say that tips don't work—sometimes they do.

Q: We've been talking for quite a while now, and I see that the markets are closing. So it's almost time for you to "start" your working day. But we still haven't covered what happens between the time that you finish marking up your trading sheet and the opening of the markets the next day, where you're buying or selling futures contracts.

SK: Well, after I finish marking my trading sheet, I scrutinize the right-hand column, "Take Action," and note what I want to buy or sell for the following day and what my price limits should be. Then I enter the following day's orders on a large brokers' buy/sell pad and leave the completed page on my desk. My assistant comes in early every morning and enters my various buy and sell orders with the respective brokers and floors. As I said, by the time I arrive at the office, my orders are all in and my day is half over . . .

Q: . . . that is, until 3 o'clock in the afternoon, when it starts again.

SK: Yes, that's right. But it's a living.

The Most Important Chapter in the Book

4

This may be the most important chapter in the book—it should really be printed in extra-large type. It's about *keeping losses small.*

When I first entered the commodity business in 1960, the first lesson I learned was, "Cut your losses and let your profits run." This was granted such importance that I always sagely offered it to my clients and associates. And, interestingly enough, everyone was always giving me the same free advice. Naturally, it was prominently stated in every trading guide and manual I've ever read.

So, the $64 question is this: If everyone gives this advice and knows how important it is, how come hardly anyone ever follows it? I mean, *really follows it,* not just talks about following it.

Since 1960, I've spoken to hundreds of speculators about their commodity trading. Most of them were consistent losers, many in a substantial way. My final query was always specific: "If you had limited all losses to 45 percent of each position's margin, what would your final results have been?" (In this calculation, allowance had to be made for those profitable close-outs which would have been liquidated unprofitably on the basis of our stated 45 percent margin loss limitation.)

The results of my unofficial poll were hardly surprising. In all cases the profitability would have been vastly improved, and in many situations the final result would have been an overall profit. Here's an actual case, based on personal experience.

The Penton Corporation, a client of mine, was formed in January 1969 with $105,000 capital, for the purpose of trading commodities. In October, just nine months later, Penton stopped trading after having lost its original $105,000 plus an additional $30,000.

A breakdown of Penton's trades reveals the following:

Profitable trades	12	Average size of profit	$1,799
Losing trades	23	Average size of loss	$6,844

Some trading record, isn't it? Interestingly enough, though, if Penton had limited losses to just 45 percent of the margin on each position, the results would have been far different:

Profitable trades	12	Average size of profit	$1,799
Losing trades	23	Average size of loss	$1,340

In summary, instead of having lost $135,000 in trading, Penton would have been out only $9,232. What a difference!

Lest you feel that this sort of financial indigestion happens only to nonprofessional speculators, let me tell you about another account. This was an experienced, sophisticated Swiss bank, with its own commodity trading department. The account was opened in February 1969 and closed in March of the following year. Final trading results: a loss of $45,500. Here is a summary of the thirteen months' operation:

Profitable trades	3	Average size of profit	$ 255
Losing trades	11	Average size of loss	$4,156

Let's see how the bank would have fared had losses been limited to 45 percent of each position's margin:

Profitable trades	3	Average size of profit	$255
Losing trades	11	Average size of loss	$634

Predictably, a far different picture: the bank would have lost $6,719 instead of $45,500.

It is particularly enlightening to compare Penton's and the bank's trading results with those of my own Commodity Management Services (CMS), established in July 1971 with $18,000 capital. On December 31, 1972, after eighteen months of trading, CMSs capital had appreciated to $130,000. Here's a summary of the trading:

Total number of closed-out trades	230
Number of trades closed out at a profit	150
Number of trades closed out at a loss	80
Average size of profit	$1,020
Average size of loss	$ 515

These three trading recaps tell the story. Both Penton and the bank tended to trade *against* the major trends and made no attempt to limit losses on adverse positions. On the contrary, profitable positions were quickly closed out, while losses were held (for what? for even bigger losses!). CMS, on the other hand, was obviously predisposed to trade *with* the prevailing major market trend (65 percent of all trades were profitable) and followed a policy of minimizing losses and allowing profits to run (the average profit was twice the average loss).

CMS's excellent trading record attracted some attention in Wall Street, and a number of individuals and institutions became interested in our market performance for CMS and others. One such person was Alex, an international banker who represented investment and commercial interests in Europe and the Middle East. Alex's bank and its affiliates had been involved in commodity dealings for more than forty years, and they were interested in our approach to timing trades. He asked me to prepare a brief (he stressed brief) memorandum summarizing our approach to trade timing. Here's what I sent him:

I. *On Initiating a Position*
   Trade in the direction of the major trend, against the minor trend. For example, *if the major trend is clearly up,* trade the market from the long side, or not at all, buying when:
   a. the minor trend has turned down, *and*
   b. prices are "digging" into support, *and*
   c. the market has made a 35–50 percent retracement of the previous up leg.
   If the major trend is clearly down trade the market from the short side, or not at all, selling when:
   a. the minor trend has turned up, *and*
   b. prices have advanced into overhead resistance, *and*

      c. the market has made a 35–50 percent retracement of the previous down leg.

II. *On Closing Out a Position*

      a. *At a profit.* Liquidate one-third of the position at a logical (chart) price objective into overhead resistance (for a long position) or into underlying support (for a short position).* Liquidate another third at a long-term (chart) price objective into major resistance or support. Protect the remaining third with stop orders, advancing the stop as the market moves favorably. Eventually the position will be stopped out, but perhaps at a far greater profit than was originally anticipated.

      b. *At a loss.* There are, basically, three approaches:

        1. Enter an arbitrary "money" stop-loss; e.g., 40–50 percent of the margin deposit.

        2. Enter a chart-point stop-loss; i.e., to close out the position when the *major trend* reverses against your position—not when the *minor trend* reverses (that's just the point where you should be *initiating* the position, not closing it out).

        3. Maintain the position until you are convinced that you are wrong (the *major trend* has reversed against you) and then close out on the first technical correction.†

Shortly after receiving this memo, Alex proposed a meeting. It was ostensibly to discuss commodity trading in general, but the subject of minimizing losses without commensurately reducing profits dominated the meeting. (Apparently international bankers, too, find this a major problem in their commodity trading operations.) Present were Alex and one of his traders, Porridge; Slam, who works for me as a commodity analyst; and myself. Here's how it went:

SK: The problem isn't how to get the big profits. Big profits are inherent in commodity trading; but so are big losses, and the problem is how to avoid *them*. It's virtually impossible to be a big winner without some practical approach, some system, for keeping the inevitable losses to a minimum.

---

* Following this first liquidation, be alert to reinstate the position, or even 1.5 times the liquidated position, on a subsequent technical correction, as outlined in the above discussion, "On Initiating a Position."

† There are substantial dangers to this particular approach, which will be discussed later in this chapter.

PORRIDGE: I think that on most of our losing trades we stay with the position much too long, and that's where our big losses—the really ruinous ones—develop. I suppose that when we initiate a trade, either long or short, we should predetermine how much we are willing to lose, and either stop out or just liquidate the position at that point.

ALEX: Should that exit point be some percentage of the margin deposit, or some particular price level, either a chart stop-loss or some mechanical-system stop point?

SLAM: Well, as a general proposition, I don't think you should ever lose more than 40 to 50 percent of the margin deposit—for example, not more than $2000 in silver or $750 in wheat. If there's an efficient chart stop-loss point, where the major trend will have clearly reversed, and if the market is broad enough to take the stops, you should stop out at that point. If there isn't a logical chart stop point within an acceptable loss limit (40 to 50 percent of margin), then perhaps you should arbitrarily stop out the position when the loss reaches that point. Look, you can always get back in if the market shows you that you closed out prematurely.

SK: That's fine when you're talking about a small position. But how do you get out of a large position—say a 200- or 300-contract copper position—when the market's against you by 45 percent of your margin? Anyone can get out of 5 or 10 contracts, but how do you get out of the big one?

SLAM: Look, you still must have some way of limiting your losses.

ALEX: Sure, sure, but closing out a big position—like the kind we're inclined to carry—on a chart stop-loss means that we're invariably buying on strength and selling on weakness. We've had some awfully bad experiences trading like that. Really, there must be some better approach.

SK: Yes, there is a better approach. First of all, let's consider the problem of losing trades. I think the main cause of losing trades is that one has been downright careless or sloppy in initiating the position. Right? How frequently does a speculator put on a position—even a large one—for no better reason than he was bored or tired of waiting for his price, or because of a tip or some gossip on the news tape, or merely because the market started moving and he was afraid he'd miss the move? Look, we're usually wrong when we trade for any of those reasons.

ALEX: I'll buy that logic. That's been our experience, too. But go on, develop that idea further.

SK: Well, assuming we've put on the position properly—and my recent memo to you outlined my thoughts on that—if the market immediately starts to move our way, we should ensure that we don't permit a good profit to turn into a loss. I mean, if we have a paper profit of, say, 50 percent of the margin, we should arbitrarily close out the position on a no-loss stop basis. We've

Commodity Chart Service, Commodity Research Bureau Inc.

Figure 9.

Any short position in June cattle, sold on the break below 46.00 (A) should have been protected with buy stops in the 44.00 to 45.00 level (B).

all watched too many really good profits turn into losses, and ultimately into sizable losses. Look at these charts.* There's absolutely no excuse to permit that to happen.

PORRIDGE: Yes, quite true. But what about those positions which start moving against you from the beginning?

SLAM: If you've timed the trade well—that is, bought on a good reaction within a major uptrend, or sold on a strong rally within a major downtrend—you probably wouldn't be justified in abandoning the position until *the major trend actually turned against you.* We handle this, really, in either of two ways:

Commodity Chart Service, Commodity Research Bureau Inc.

Figure 10.

Long positions in July plywood, bought on the major breakout at the 150.00 level (C), should have been protected with sell stops between 150.00 and 155.00 ((D).

* See Figures 9 and 10.

1. We'll watch the intraday market action, and if toward the close it appears that the major trend has reversed (or is reversing), we'll bang out all, or at least part, of the position right near the close.

2. On the other hand, if the market is at what appears to be a major bottom area, in good support, and other technical or fundamental indicators continue to advise holding the long position, we may sit with it. We certainly won't add to the position, though, and we keep an open mind on the advisability of closing out on the next rally into overhead.

ALEX: But aren't you taking the risk that the market won't rally to give you a chance to bail out—what if it goes against you and keeps on going?

SK: Yes, and there we are, still sitting with the position. Of course that's always a possibility. That's why we're so careful in such a situation. I'll tell you that we're generally not inclined to take that route when we're short and "see" an upside breakout. Those upside thrusts tend to be violent, and we'd rather cover the short position on the day the market first *closes* on the upside breakout, than wait and hope for a reaction. But after an extended bear market, where prices have reached or even surpassed our major downside "count," and where the market is finding good long-term buying support, we may decide to sit through the downturn. Sure, we might get stuck with it—but, on the other hand, the market might very well turn up after cleaning up stops underlying the market.

I neither saw nor heard from Alex for three weeks after that meeting. Just about the time I was starting to wonder why I hadn't heard from him—had I left him so unimpressed?—he came walking into my office one morning. He left about an hour later, but not before saying some flattering things about our trading strategy, and how we had helped him and Porridge reevaluate and improve the bank's trading approach. Oh, he also gave us a few good accounts to manage, as a bonus.

Just one more word on the subject of keeping losses small. What can happen if you don't control your losses—do you just lose money? Well, sometimes you lose more than money, as was expressed in a letter I received several years ago.

NOVEMBER 8TH, 1967

KROLL, DALON & COMPANY., INC.
25 BROAD ST.
NEW YORK, N.Y. 10004

GENTLEMEN:

A NEW YORK FRIEND SENT ME YOUR WORLD SUGAR MARKET LETTER OF OCTOBER 17TH., WHICH I FOUND INTERESTING AND SUBSEQUENTLY QUITE PROFITABLE AS IT RE-ENFORCED MY FEELINGS ON THE BULLISH SIDE.

THE QUOTATION FROM JESSE LIVERMORE REMINDED ME OF MY LATE LAMENTED FATHER, WHEN I ASKED HIM AS A BOY, HOW YOU MADE MONEY ON THE FUTURES MARKET. HIS ANSWER, "YOU HAVE TO BE BOLD AND YOU HAVE TO BE RIGHT." I THEN SAID, "WHAT IF YOU ARE BOLD AND WRONG," AND HE SAID, "YOU JUST GO DOWN WITH THE SHIP." HE DID JUST THAT, UNFORTUNATELY. . . .

The Copper Caper—How We're Going
to Make a Million

COPPER (kop'ər), n. 1. *Chem.* a malleable,
ductile, metallic element having a character-
istic reddish-brown color; used in large
quantities as an electrical conductor and in
the manufacture of alloys, as brass and
bronze.

*—The Random House Dictionary
of the English Language*

5

There are any number of Wall Street hero books, about how
someone made a million in common stocks or doubled his money
in convertible bonds. There are even books about how someone
lost a fortune or did some other dumb thing like that. I've often
wondered why someone doesn't write about how he's *going* to
make the million, before he does it. Then let him share with the
reader the progress of the game and its many facets—the planning,
the hope, the worry and anxiety, the triumph and despair, because the road to a million dollars is paved with all those feelings
whether one makes it or not.

Let's live it as he lives it—let's see why he believes it will work,
how he plans the entire campaign, step by uneasy step, and
finally let's see what actually happens. Even if he's wrong—if he
took the shot and missed—let's examine why it didn't work. Let's
live through the errors and miscalculations, and examine what was
done (or should have been done) to minimize the ensuing disaster.

Let's do it!

In early November 1972, Snap and his sidekick, Crackle, were
lounging in my office crowing about our just-closed-out cotton
trade. It was quite a coup, we all agreed. We had bought a large
cotton position in August and September, between 27.00 to 28.50
for December and 27.50 to 28.00 for March, and had just sold

out the entire 190-contract position for an average 200-point profit. This amounted to a profit of just under $200,000, in less than 3 months.

Snap was looking for an encore and was starting to talk about shorting May potatoes, then trading around 5.60. Snap fancies himself quite the potato trader—his game is to sell them on the way up or buy them on the way down, it doesn't matter which. He sometimes breaks even, but usually he doesn't.

"Look," I said, "aren't you guys tired of fooling around, of scalping trades and getting stopped in and out of every position, of selling short the front end of every major bull market in sight? Let's change the game plan. Let's make the next play a real biggie—for a real big score. How are we going to do it? We're going to buy copper futures—oodles and oodles of copper futures —and we'll sell the whole position next year for a 20-cent profit. That's how we'll do it!"

I could feel a big move for copper in every bone in my body, and I was ready to bet big on it. Here's why:

Copper was currently trading near its lowest price levels since 1965, with No. 2 scrap at 35¢ per pound, and nearby futures on the Comex at 46¢. Surprisingly enough, of all the commodities traded on U.S. and Canadian exchanges—and that covers some 30 commodities—copper was the only one selling at its lowest levels of the last decade. *The only one.*

The copper market had substantially reached its major downside count objective and was currently finding powerful long-term buying support at the 45¢ to 46¢ level. Furthermore, a study of copper's long-term price cycles suggested that we were due for a major bull market. (See Figure 11.) Since 1964 we'd had bull markets in copper every 2 years, as follows:

Bull Mkt Year	Price Level From Which Bull Mkt Started	Bull Mkt High	Extent of Price Move
1964	30.00¢	62.00¢	32¢
1966	38.00¢	82.00¢	44¢
1968	42.00¢	76.00¢	34¢
1970	44.00¢	78.00¢	34¢
1973*	44.00¢	72.00¢†	28¢

* Projected bull market for the coming year, i.e., 1973.
† This is my minimum long-term price objective.

The fundamental market situation, too, supported this bullish view. Among the significant short-term factors:

1. Consumer copper inventories were at relatively low levels. Although warehouse copper stocks in London, New York, and

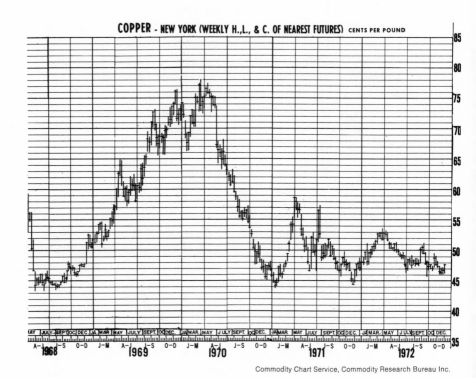

COPPER - NEW YORK (WEEKLY H.,L., & C. OF NEAREST FUTURES) CENTS PER POUND

Commodity Chart Service, Commodity Research Bureau Inc.

Figure 11.

Japan were quite high—and this was cited as the main bearish element—an anticipated worldwide industrial pickup, with its concomitant increase in copper demand, should reduce warehouse stocks and put upward pressure on prices.

2. Historically, there is a time lag of six months to a year be-

tween general economic recovery and the response of increased copper demand. The lack of strong demand during the past six to twelve months, therefore, was not unexpected. Indications of greatly increased usage were just now becoming evident.

3. Strong inflationary price trends, which had affected all other commodities, should begin to exert upward price pressure on both newly mined and scrap copper.

Longer-term bullish market factors included:

1. The underlying long-term trend in world copper demand was rising and should continue to rise. Copper is an indispensable element in the generation and transmission of electrical energy, and total production and usage of electrical energy was rising much faster than world population, particularly in the emerging nations.

2. The required capital investment per ton of production was rising sharply, greatly increasing the overall costs of copper production. In addition, control of operations in major producing areas, such as South America, was moving into less experienced and less capitalized hands.

3. A new force had recently emerged which, at least for the next few years, should bring about a change in the economics of the entire copper industry: a growing shortage of modern, efficient smelting facilities. This was largely due to today's preoccupation with air pollution and ecology, where large amounts of capital will be required to "clean up" the smelting operations, and where older, less efficient facilities might be taken out of operation rather than being modernized at substantial cost.

Snap and Crackle were very enthusiastic, particularly since they shared my bullish copper view. My plan was really simple; in Wall Street, the simplest schemes are frequently the most effective (and the most profitable, too).

For the past few weeks I had been nibbling at the long side of copper, buying small positions in March and May futures for my managed accounts and myself. Now I would begin buying in earnest, at the 47.60 level for March 1973 and around 48.30 for May 1973. Since the major trend was still sideways to down—although I "saw" a clear and fairly imminent reversal—I would keep the position down to about 150 contracts, waiting for the trend to turn up before buying my next increment.

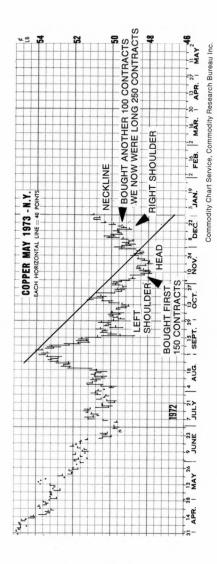

Figure 12.

Commodity Chart Service, Commodity Research Bureau Inc.

On November 15, 1972, I wrote the following analysis:

The major trend is still sideways to down, with the minor trend up. The market should find strong buying support at the 48.00 level, basis May, and resistance between 49.00 and 50.00. The first rally from a major bear market rarely holds, and I would expect some downward price reaction from this 50.00 resistance level. *I would use this reaction as a buying opportunity,* doubling up on our long position on a 50 percent reaction to the 49.00 to 49.50 level.*

I furthermore see a possible head-and-shoulders bottom developing, with the 50.50 to 51.00 resistance level forming the neckline; any reaction from that point should find solid buying support between 49.00 and 49.50, corresponding to the right shoulder. From that level, I would expect renewed market strength, with an advance likely back to and through the 50.50 to 51.00 (neckline) level. This 51.00 upside breakout would complete the major bottom formation and would establish a minimum near-term price objective of 54.00, which should provide nothing more than temporary resistance.

I expect copper to develop into a major bull market, and for the longer term I project a minimum major price objective of 70.00¢ to 75.00¢.

The market, essentially, followed my script. On December 18, 19, and 20, the May future traded between 48.90 and 49.70, affording us the opportunity (as expressed in my memo) to add to the position. We picked up 100-odd contracts on this reaction, bringing our *starting position* to just over 250 contracts, at an average price of 49.50.

My game plan now calls for us to maintain the long position, adding *carefully and patiently* on reactions into support, and ultimately accumulating a total long position of some 400 contracts.

For the final thrilling episode of the Copper Caper, see Chapter 7.

The following table summarizes the longer-term profit possibilities of this Copper Caper:

* See Figure 12.

Number of Contracts Held

Price Move	1	100	200	250	300	400	500
1¢	$ 250	$ 25,000	$ 50,000	$ 62,500	$ 75,000	$ 100,000	$ 125,000
5¢	1,250	125,000	250,000	312,500	375,000	500,000	725,000
10¢	2,500	250,000	500,000	625,000	750,000	1,000,000	1,250,000
15¢	3,750	375,000	750,000	937,500	1,125,000	1,500,000	1,975,000
20¢	5,000	500,000	1,000,000	1,250,000	1,500,000	2,000,000	2,500,000
25¢	6,250	625,000	1,250,000	1,562,500	1,875,000	2,500,000	3,125,000

And Here's to You, Jesse Livermore

The more things change, the more they remain the same.

—Alphonse Karr

6

I once observed my daughter Laura reading a familiar book—
I think it was *Black Beauty.* "Haven't I seen you with that book before?" I asked. Laura replied that this was her fifth reading.

I remember wondering if I'd ever find any book so interesting
and meaningful that I'd want to read it five times. Yet, in writing
this book, I realized that there is a volume which I have read
that many times—and will undoubtedly read again. It's the most
important and valuable Wall Street book I've ever come across,
and it has influenced me significantly.

The book is *Reminiscences of a Stock Operator,* by Edwin
Lefevre, and it was published in June 1923. Although presented
in fictional form, it parallels the career of one of the greatest of
the Wall Street speculators and financial operators in both stocks
and commodities: Jesse Livermore. In many ways, trading tactics
and strategy haven't changed much since Livermore's day.

During my fifteen years in commodities I've suffered my
share (and maybe even more) of tactical errors, miscalculations,
fiascos, and outright disasters, and I've always tried to learn from
each of them. But I've enjoyed an advantage; I discovered
Reminiscences early in my career, and so had not only my own
mistakes to learn from; I also had Livermore's. And he made some

41

beauties! Fortunately for me (and for you), Lefevre analyzes them in a constructive and articulate style. For example:

> Studying my winning plays in Fullerton's office I discovered that although I often was 100 percent right on the market—I was not making as much money as my market "rightness" entitled me to. Why wasn't I?
>
> First of all, I had been bullish from the very start of a bull market, and I had backed my opinion by buying stocks. An advance followed, as I had clearly foreseen. So far, all very well. But, what else did I do? Why, I listened to the elder statesmen, and curbed my youthful impetuousness. I made up my mind to be wise and play carefully, conservatively. Everybody knows that the way to do that was to take profits and buy back your stocks on reactions. And that is precisely what I did, or rather what I tried to do; for I often took profits and waited for a reaction that never came. And I saw my stock go kiting up ten points more and I sitting there with my four-point profit safe in my conservative pocket. They say you never grow poor taking profits. No, you don't. But, neither do you grow rich taking a four-point profit in a bull market.
>
> Where I should have made twenty thousand dollars, I made two thousand. That was what my conservatism did for me.

And here's one of my favorite quotations. I keep this one, typed on a small card, in my top desk drawer:

> . . . After spending many years in Wall Street and after making and losing millions of dollars, I want to tell you this: It never was my thinking that made the big money for me. It was always my sitting. Got that? My sitting tight. It is no trick at all to be right on the market. You always find lots of early bulls in bull markets and lots of early bears in bear markets. I have known many men who were right at exactly the right time, and began buying or selling stocks when prices were at the very level which should show the greatest profit. And their experience invariably matched mine; that is, they made no real money out of it. Men who can both be right and sit tight are uncommon. I found it one of the hardest things to learn. But it is only after a stock operator has firmly grasped this that he can make big money. It is literally true that millions come easier to a trader after he knows how to trade than hundreds did in the days of his ignorance.

I must have bought and given away 40 or 50 copies of this book, starting in 1961. Who got the first copy? I remember that clearly. I gave the first copy to Paul, one of my earliest and most memorable commodity clients.

It was Paul's first commodity trade, and he bought 10,000 bushels (two contracts) of May soybeans at 2.25 in November 1960. By the time May beans hit 3.35 in April of the following year, he had pyramided his original $5,000 and two contracts into some $80,000 and 45 contracts. What a bonanza, especially for a first-time commodity trader! But as the market kept advancing, Paul got progressively more bullish. His original price objective was 2.85, then 3.20, and by the time it got to 3.35 he was talking about 4.00 beans.

His equity topped out at $80,000. Just a few days (and a $30,000 decrease in equity) later, I tried to persuade Paul to close out. "You've got $50,000 left—more than you ever imagined it would be. Close out now, and take a trip around the world," I told him. But Paul was smarting from the last market drop; he would make that $30,000 back and then close out.

The story has a familiar ending—it happens all the time. Paul's remaining $50,000 rapidly disappeared, leaving him with little more than carfare back to the Bronx (some "ride") and the copy of *Reminiscences* I had given him (he should have read it). As a matter of fact, when he tallied up his misadventure, he found that he had suffered a net loss of $7,000, or $2,000 more than his original investment.

I highly recommend that, after you finish reading this book, you read *Reminiscences*. Perhaps you will be able to salvage $50,000 from your next bull-market position.

Update on the Copper Caper—It Worked!

7

Riding a winning commodity position is a lot like riding a bucking bronco. Once you manage to get aboard, you know what you have to do—hang on and stay hung on; not get bumped or knocked off till the end of the ride. And you know that if you can just manage to stay in the saddle, you're a winner. Sounds simple? Well, that's the essence of successful trading.

No doubt about it, a speculator's worst enemy is himself. After all, what should be so difficult about doing nothing? That is, not trading at all—not at all.

I knew we were on the right track in copper because the action of the market told me we were right. The price was moving up smartly, out of the long-term base support area. And on the rise, both open interest and trading volume were expanding—a bullish action. Rallies were longer and stronger, reactions were shorter and weaker.

All I had to do was ignore the pit gossip, the market letters and commentators, and even the news. Why ignore the news? Because to a great extent the price makes the news, and not vice versa.

I once bet a friend that I could predict the news (we were following cocoa) by observing the price fluctuations, and it worked. A strong market was invariably followed by bullish news, and a weak market by bearish news. For instance, there's that pesky little capsid bug that every few years does nasty things on cocoa beans in storage—but the foul fellow exhibits an uncanny sense of timing: it does its thing only during bull markets. And I've observed, from time to time, substantial stocks of "previously undiscovered" cocoa beans being suddenly (and unexpectedly, of course) found in a cocoa warehouse somewhere—but this seems to occur only during long bear markets. Coincidence? Hardly, I believe. The futures market, as expressed by the price, is a super-sensitive barometer which discounts most of the news before it is generally known to the public speculator.

So there we were, sitting long some 250 copper contracts. The news was invariably bullish on up days and bearish on down days. My biggest problem was to restrain myself from buying on the up moves and selling on the reactions. It sure was a problem. I invented little devices to keep myself from trading: I got up a little early every morning and read portions from *Reminiscenses,* especially the part about Livermore's having made his big money "sitting." I carried the book with me and would leave it on my desk during the trading day, right in front of my direct phone to the floor.

I projected a major price objective of 70.00 to 75.00¢. My game would be to trade in the direction of the major trend (by being long) *and* against the minor trend (by buying on minor reactions, especially on the third or fourth day of the reaction, if trading volume was drying up). Finally, I would have to resist all temptations (and there were many) to scalp, day-trade, or sell out on reactions because of a bearish tip or rumor.

So I bought more Mays and Julys on January 3 around the 51.00¢ level (basis May), more on the week-long reaction on January 17 and 18 between 52.50 and 53.00¢ and our final increment on the gap opening at 57.00¢ on the morning of February 13.

That now brought our position up to 350 contracts. Enough.

On February 22 the market opened on a 200-point upside gap, closing the day up by the limit at 60.60¢ for May. This strong opening gap was a clear tip-off, portending a bullish market. It looked to me like a midpoint gap; the market had already advanced some 12.00¢, from 48.00¢ to 60.00¢, so I projected another 12.00¢ on the upside. This 72.00¢ price objective coincided with my original price objective from the base formation. I am always pleased (and impressed) when I can come up with two or more unrelated price counts, each independently projecting approximately the same objective. In this situation, my two counts to the 72.00¢ level were augmented by still another important technical indicator: the market would encounter strong long-term overhead resistance between 70.00 and 75.00¢ which should halt the advance, at least temporarily.

Well, between February 23 and March 2, copper futures advanced some 8.00¢. We were still carrying the 350 contracts, and each 1.00¢ price advance represented an equity increase of $87,-500. What a move! Despite assurances to myself, I realized that I was getting nervous (and impatient, too) carrying such a large one-sided position. Although it still seemed too early to sell out, I thought this a good time to begin shifting to a less risky bullish position—via switches.*

An important feature of most major copper bull markets is a price inversion by which, because of shortages of spot supplies, nearby futures gain relative to more distant futures and eventually sell at substantial premiums. I was watching the switch differentials closely for the first clue of an impending inversion. (Figure 13.)

On March 1, May copper closed higher than July for the first time, and on the following day I breathed a long sigh of relief, sold out 100 long Mays, and put on 200 switches; that is, I bought 100 Julys and 100 Septembers versus the sale of 200 Decembers.

I had now hedged our bet somewhat, by taking profits on 100 outright long contracts and putting on 200 new switch positions. My rationale for the switches was that if the market advanced, the nearby Julys and Septembers would advance faster than the Decembers (the switch would widen), whereas if the market declined, the nearbys would decline less than the short Decembers.

I had another reason for selling out 30 percent of the outright long position and putting on less risky switches: the market had

* Also known as straddles or spreads.

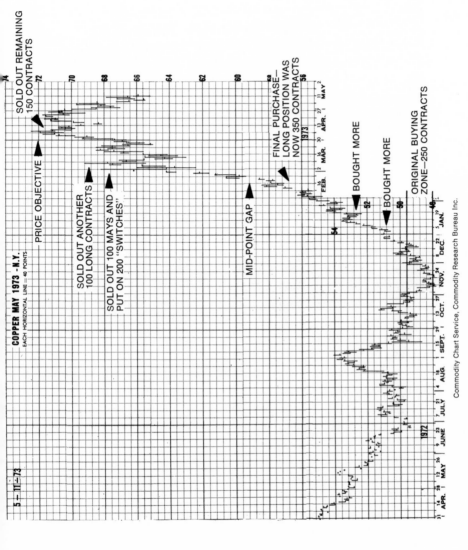

Figure 13.

Commodity Chart Service, Commodity Research Bureau Inc.

advanced substantially, and, at the 68.00 level, was beginning to approach my long-term price objective. I anticipated a more volatile, wider-swinging market from here, and I wanted to position myself to capitalize on the price swings. Specifically, on a further extension of the bull move I would scale out the remaining 250 long contracts, maintaining the 200-contract switch position. On the other hand, if the market declined sharply I would begin covering the short (December) leg of the switch position.

As anticipated, the market was wide-swinging, and I adhered to my game plan. On the early-March rally to 68.00–69.00¢, I sold out another 100 Mays and Julys from the original long position, holding the switches intact. This brought the long position down to 150 contracts. I had sold down to a "sleeping level."

Toward the end of March the market reacted downward, and I covered 120 of the 200 short Decembers from the switch position, between 63.00 and 64.00¢, holding the long leg of the switches intact. From there the market rallied, and during the beginning of April I sold out the 120 long Julys and Septembers from the switch position, between 67.50 and 70.50, basis July.

The balance of the move was over before I knew it. That's one of the unique aspects of commodity trading. You project a major price move, either up or down, and calculate the likely extent and timing of the move. If you're right, you'll invariably find that the move takes place much quicker than anticipated. Commodity markets really get to their next level fast, really fast.

Anyway, May copper reached 72.45¢ on the morning of April 9 and weakened during the session, closing on the lows at 71.15¢. I banged out the remaining 150-contract long position that day, because:

1. The market had attained my major upside price objective and was coming into heavy long-term overhead resistance.

2. Prices had registered life-of-contract highs and then seemed to stall. This wasn't bullish action, and as the day proceeded it became apparent that the market was apt to close on the day's lows. A decisive trend reversal, if I've ever seen one.

In view of Factors 1 and 2 above, I viewed the market as being particularly vulnerable. The sidelines seemed the best place to be. After banging out the balance of the net long position on April 9,

I eased out of the remaining switches during the next few days.

When we tallied up the entire Copper Caper, we found that we had taken an average of 15¢ out of 350 contracts, plus another 1¢ to 2¢ out of the 200 switches. Even after commissions, it tallied a million dollars plus. A neat half year's work!

If You Think Cocoa Is Treacherous,
Try Platinum

8

Adam Smith, in *The Money Game,* said that whenever he had the urge to trade cocoa, he'd go lie down until the feeling passed. I happen to agree with him on cocoa—only I'd add platinum to the list.

One of the real luxuries that attracted me to the commodity business is that I can concentrate on following just a dozen or so commodities, essentially the same ones year after year. So, since 1960 I've been tracking such commodities as wheat, corn, soybeans, and pork bellies in Chicago, and copper, sugar, and silver in New York—plus a few markets in London.

Platinum has been on my tracking list, too, and I've always attributed its inclusion to some innate masochistic tendency. Not that I haven't made money in platinum over the years. It's just that I've had to work (and suffer) harder for my platinum profits than for the others. My platinum positions have generally been on the right side of the market, and I've accumulated substantial paper profits on many occasions. But funny things always happened to me on the way to the bank—the profits seemed to erode just before I was ready to cash in.

The last time was in February 1971, when I had carefully and patiently accumulated a large position in July platinum around the 106.00 level. The market got up to 118.00—I had scale-up sell orders starting around 119.60, and right before I got my sell orders off, the market just collapsed. It didn't slide, erode, decline, or merely go down. Oh no, it just disintegrated, right down to 96.00. In retrospect I consider myself fortunate in having gotten out of the entire position on the next rally, with just a commission loss.

Well, it's now the first week in February 1973, and platinum is starting to wiggle provocatively. When I saw myself beginning to yield to the platinum fever, I decided to follow my higher instincts. Lying down didn't seem appropriate, so I picked up my coat and umbrella (it was raining) and wandered over to the South Street Seaport. A walk on the piers would cure me of the platinum urge. But I was wrong, because the next day the buy drums were beating louder than ever. Here we go again. . . .

Before initiating any trades I wrote up my usual memo (to myself) summarizing the platinum situation both technically and fundamentally. Here's what I wrote:

Platinum—Current Technical Situation—February 5, 1973: The major trend is up to sideways, with the minor trend down.* The minor trend turns up on a close over 150.00, basis July, while a close over 156.00 will confirm a major uptrend. I would expect good buying support in the 138.00–143.00 area, with overhead resistance between 148.00 and 152.00.

The market is being contained within a seven-month symmetrical triangle, which I view as a bullish consolidation pattern. A breakout over 156.00 would confirm this bullish view, particularly if the move was accompanied by high volume (over 1,500) *and* an expansion of open interest to over 8,000 contracts.

Conclusion: (1) Buy first increment on any setback to 143.00 level; (2) Buy second increment "on stop" at 149.00 (above the downtrend line and the recent 147.00 trading high); and (3) Buy third increment on any reaction to 154.00 following a close above 166.00.

Current Fundamental Situation: The Federal Clean Air Act of 1970 requires that, beginning with the 1975 model year, every automobile must have an approved exhaust control device. Although various exhaust systems have been explored, the platinum-based catalytic converter is currently the leading candidate. Its technical merits are well

---

* This is encouraging. As stated previously, I prefer to trade in the direction of the major trend *and* against the minor trend. In this case, the major trend is bullish and the minor trend down. Chalk one up for the buy side. (See Figure 14.)

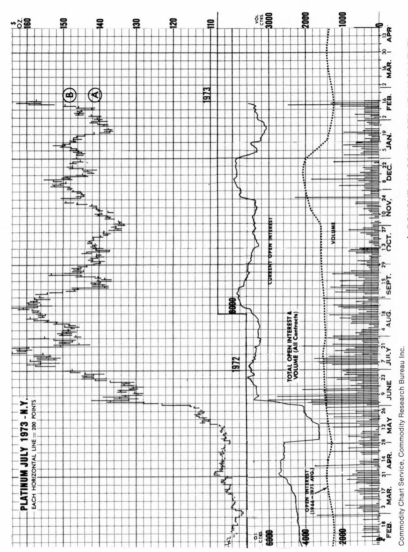

Figure 14.

I'm now projecting a rally to the 166.00 level, or higher. Following this close over 166.00, I plan to buy another 100 contracts on a reaction to the 154.00 level.

documented and its acceptance by the automobile industry appears to be increasing. The start-up time for 1975-model cars is about a year away and, although automobile manufacturers are trying to delay Federal pollution-control regulations, they are also preparing to meet these standards if Federal guidelines can't be deferred. As an example, Ford concluded arrangements with Matthey Bishop and also with W. R. Grace to supplement its earlier contract with Engelhard Industries, thus assuring them an adequate and continuing supply of the metal. It is estimated that each automobile catalytic converter would require approximately one-tenth of an ounce of platinum. Assuming an annual production of ten million cars, this would add one million ounces per annum to platinum consumption.

Other major industrial applications lie in the petroleum and chemical industries, where platinum's great value as a chemical catalyst seems to assure a healthy increase in consumption, at least over the next few years.

Finally, in addition to platinum's expanding industrial applications, one should not overlook its potential speculative demand as a "hoarding commodity." During periods of international monetary uncertainty and the accompanying flight out of paper currency into precious metals, platinum demand is likely to remain high.

Conclusion: The underlying fundamentals support this bullish view. I would expect a steady increase in demand over the next few years. Supply is not likely to keep pace with demand at current price levels; it is likely that a significant price increase will be necessary to bring out a corresponding increase in supplies.

Well, that's the situation.

Here's how we played it.*

1. On Friday, February 9, and Monday, February 12, July platinum traded between 141.50 and 146.00. We bought approximately 100 Julys and Octobers basis 143.00 for July.

2. As anticipated, the market found solid buying support at the 138.00–143.00 level and rallied smartly. On February 13, July platinum closed at 149.50. In accordance with the plan, I bought an additional 100 Julys and Octobers.

By now I had accumulated two-thirds of what I wanted to buy. I didn't want to exceed about 300 contracts; my memories of previous market debacles were vivid.

The market is acting well so far (it seems I'm always waiting

* See "Conclusion," page 51.

for the other shoe to drop when I trade platinum), volume and open interest are expanding on the rallies, and I'm looking for higher prices.

My game plan now calls for us to stand aside, letting the market rally as it will. However, on any close above 166.00 I would expect the subsequent reaction to get support around 154.00, and I'll buy another 100 contracts on that reaction. Following this, I look for an eventual move to the 195.00–205.00 level, at which point I will liquidate the position. (To be continued in Chapter 14.)

Buy High, Sell Low. "How Come We Always Lose?"

9

I suppose I should be accustomed to it by now, after all these years, but I'm not. Still have trouble figuring it out.

Why do they always get bullish on the way up and bearish on the way down? Want to know the speculators' marching song? It's "Buy High, Sell Low."

My last play in silver occurred in 1972. I accumulated a good-sized position during November and December of 1971, around the 140.00 level, and some 6 months later unloaded it around 165.00. I sold out on rallies into overhead resistance at a logical upside price objective, anticipating that I'd be able to rebuy the position, *plus an additional 50 percent*, on the next reaction.

Once again I fell into the trap of selling out a winning bull-market position in order to (try to) rebuy cheaper. The market hesitated a few days and then after some choppy fluctuations it took off, with me as a sidelines spectator. With my safe 25¢ profit, I watched silver blast off for an additional 100¢. That's quite a big move *to miss*.

At first my managed-account clients were sporting about my having sold them out just before the major move. But they started getting restless around the 250.00 level. Here's a typical phone conversation:

MAC:* Do you want to buy me some silver?

  SK: Why do you ask that?

MAC: Well, I was just wondering.

  SK: Wondering what?

MAC: Wondering if you want to buy me some silver. . . .

Why were they first starting to get bullish at those levels—
250.00, 260.00, and even 270.00?

Of course I wanted to get back aboard silver. It was headed
much, much higher. But I was waiting for a "proper" buying opportunity. Being right on the major trend isn't enough; you can
be right on the market and still lose your shirt if your timing is
wrong. I was waiting for:

1. The minor trend to turn down, *with the major trend still up.*

2. The market to retrace 40 to 50 percent of its advance, with
both volume and bullish enthusiasm diminishing on the decline.

3. A decline to a logical technical support area; for example,
at a former major resistance area which had been violated by the
bull-market advance.

So I waited . . . and waited . . . and waited . . . and . . .

During this long vigil I was also stalking copper, so it was a
quiet, boring period for me. I was sorely tempted to get aboard
both markets on several occasions but somehow managed to resist.
I must have gained 10 pounds during those weeks, eating instead
of trading, but that's the price I paid for staying out of the market.

I ate my way through a 60¢ straight-up silver advance (from
210.00 to 270.00, basis May) until—Patience, thou art the prime
virtue of the successful operator—the market finally reversed. And
a classic reversal it was! On March 1, July silver closed limit-up at
268.30. On the following day July opened on an upside gap, at
274.00, and it was all downhill from there, closing on the day's
lows at 264.00. And on Monday, March 5, the market gave me a
neat little birthday present by closing limit-down. This was it—
now *all* I had to do was project where the decline would end and
buy lots of silver contracts there.

That really wasn't as difficult as it sounds, though. Perhaps I

---

* Managed Account Client.

can be accused of taking a simplistic approach to trade timing, since I do it largely on basic technical grounds. A 50 percent retracement of the bull move measured down to 220.00, basis July, which coincided with the upper range of a solid long-term support area for the spot month, at 205.00–210.00. That clinched it for me —I had two corroborating technical indicators. My buying range would be 215.00–225.00, basis July,* and I resolved to wait for the market to come to me even if it meant possibly missing it again. It's better to risk missing a market than getting in too soon, possibly getting knocked out, and then, predictably, watching from the sidelines as the market does exactly what you had originally predicted. If you have a good price objective, based on solid technical analysis and supported by prior successful technical work, then you must maintain confidence in your analysis and hold your ground. (Try not to eat too much while you're waiting, though.)

It took just two weeks for July silver to react to 220.00, and for five more weeks it remained locked between 220.00 and 230.00. This was clearly my buying opportunity, and I picked up about 125 contracts on the Comex. I didn't want to load up excessively, because the market was still on the defensive. Although I was looking for much higher prices, I preferred adding to the position when (and if) the market showed me that I was right.

Then, on April 16, July silver closed down at 221.40, and on the very next day plummeted to 211.70. Crunch . . . there went my 220.00 support level, and with it some $125,000 in equity. This break looked like a final shake-out to me, and it put spot silver (May) right back into the solid 205.00 long-term support area. Fortunately, we had plenty of funds available (the advantage of not overcommitting but instead maintaining an adequate cash reserve for such contingencies), so I tiptoed in and bought another 40 silvers around the 213.00 level, basis July.

For another 3 weeks the market traded within the 210.00–218.00 range, basis July, affording many of the fair-weather bulls an opportunity to turn bearish and sell out their long positions.†

And I even started hearing from some of my MACs again:

---

* See Figure 15.

† According to *Market Vane*, Pasadena, the bullish consensus declined to 31 percent on April 24. (See Figure 15.)

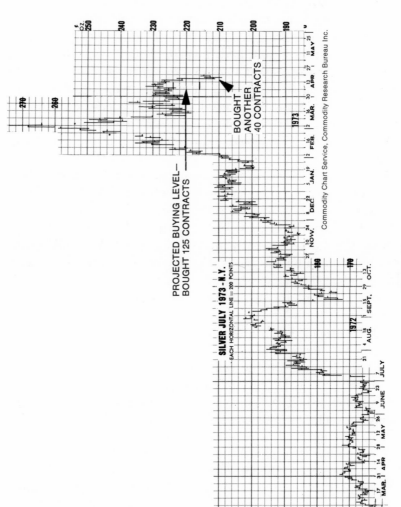

Figure 15.

MAC: Do you want to sell out my silver?

  SK: Why do you ask that?

MAC: Well, I was just wondering.

  SK: Wondering what?

MAC: Wondering if you want to sell out my silver. . . .

     Sound familiar?

So the Speculators Sold Silver; Who Bought It and Why?

10

My MACs weren't the only ones I heard from about the silver market; I also had a long conversation with Dr. G, an astute economist and senior officer of a major Swiss bank. He has spent nearly forty years in the field of precious metals and is much involved with trading them.

He was in a particularly expansive mood, and was highly amused at the "antics" of the large body of uninformed silver speculators, to whom he kept referring to as "your baby bulls" and "your baby bears."

He spoke about the international monetary situation and the Swiss bankers' attitude toward the American stock market and the precious-metals markets, then made some private predictions:

"The international monetary situation is far from settled. There's still a major distrust of paper currencies, so the natural and traditional refuge for our clients is still the precious metals.

"My clients and I have lost interest in your stock market, at least for the present. We've been liquidating some of our holdings, and generally are not committing any new money to stocks.

"Gold is going to go through the roof. And what's more, we look for much higher silver prices over the next year. The present gold-silver ratio of 40–1 makes silver quite cheap. I'm looking for this 40–1 ratio to decline."

He was skeptical concerning the widely held view that the U.S. government would be selling some 117 million ounces of stockpile silver on the open market: "First, I'm not convinced that your government has that much available silver; second, even if they do have it, I don't think they'll go through with the sale; and third, even if they do sell it, the world market will absorb it handily."

Both his bank and other foreign banks have been advising clients to buy precious metals, primarily gold and silver. They buy gold in London or Zurich, but most of their silver purchases are now being made in New York, with the bullion being shipped back to Europe. This helps account for the persistent withdrawal of New York silver stocks, and he felt that this net warehouse withdrawal would continue.

What an interesting and timely interview. It was reassuring to know that Dr. G and his associates were buying silver—I considered them most welcome shipmates.

The 210.00–218.00 three-week trading range was accompanied by reduced trading volume and a net decrease of some 6,000 contracts in the open interest. The speculative public was liquidating long positions, and the market appeared to be moving from weak to strong hands, greatly strengthening its technical condition. This impressed me as bullish action, and I accumulated another 35 silvers between 215.00 and 219.00 (basis July), bringing our total silver position to around 200 contracts.

We didn't have long to wait. Gold started moving, and silver was right behind it. On Thursday, May 3, July silver opened at 214.00 and closed limit-bid at 222.40. This rallied prices right smack into heavy overhead resistance, and by all rights the market should have reacted downward. Well, it didn't sell off; it held steady for three more days, and then, July silver closed with a bang at 228.70 on May 8, just a hair from the important 230.00 breakout level. What a bullish market! On the following day, July opened at 234.00—IT HAD BROKEN THROUGH—closing for the day at 235.30. (Figure 16.)

Gold continued strong, moving from 90.00 to 112.00 in just three weeks, while silver zoomed right up to 255.50 before profit taking and new short selling developed. When I'm long in a con-

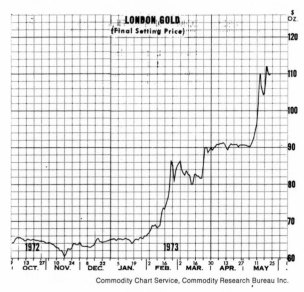

Commodity Chart Service, Commodity Research Bureau Inc.

Figure 16.

firmed major bull market, I always relish these technical reactions —they greatly strengthen the underlying tone of a market.

Then came Tuesday, May 15, a memorable day. July silver traded up to 255.40, which was limit-bid, and then plummeted during the final hours of trading straight to 236.20, limit-down. Trade interests were frantic buyers near the lows, bidding for contracts in any months they could get. I managed to pick up 10 contracts in the final minutes of trading, far fewer than I was actually bidding for.

After the smoke had cleared, the silver watchers found that the market had traded over a 20¢ range, from limit-up to limit-down for the day, with a record volume of 16,151 contracts (representing 161,510,000 troy ounces of silver) having changed hands.

What could have sparked this crazy, irrational sell-off? Why should there be this deluge of sell orders in such a strong and dynamic bull market, and on a big reaction, no less? It didn't take long to find out what happened—the story was all over the floor. One of the large commission houses had apparently flooded the pit with sell orders "at the market," touching off stop-loss sell orders of their own clients and of other public speculators. And the major

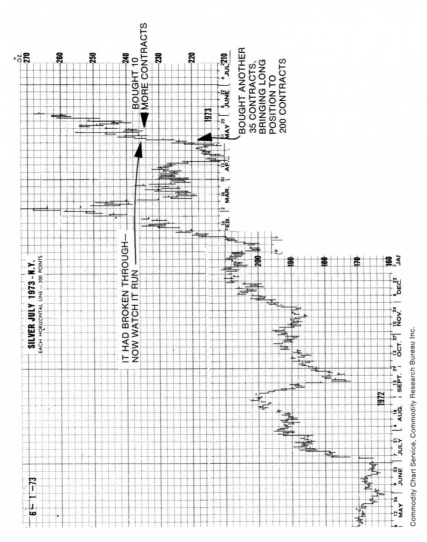

Figure 17.

Commodity Chart Service, Commodity Research Bureau Inc.

trade and floor operators were there, as usual, with a bushel basket, buying all they could get.

I took a long, hard look at the silver market the next morning. Interestingly, the previous day's reaction retraced just about 50 percent of the last up leg (the market had advanced from 210.00 to 255.00, and then reacted 20¢ down to 235.00). We were still in a major bull market, and that meant just one thing to me: *stay long*. The market looked ready to resume its advance.

And it did just that. Following its record-breaking day, the market rallied 15.00¢, back to 254.00, reacted back to test the 242.00 level, and then took off. On Friday, May 25, July silver was up 8.40¢, closing for the day at 251.20. The floor didn't know of any specific news to account for the rally, which didn't really surprise me.

But after the close that day, the Reuters news tape carried the following item:

SILVER STOCKS STILL FALLING

Washington, May 25—Industry stocks of silver as of March 31 showed a further decline, dropping to 46.0 million ounces, according to a U.S. Bureau of Mines report on silver covering first quarter, 1973.

The lower end March stock compared with holdings of 52.1 million ounces on December 31, 1972, which the Bureau revised downward from its preliminary previous estimate of 63.6 million ounces.

At the same time, the Bureau reported net industrial consumption of silver during first quarter 1973 at 48.6 million ounces, up from the 42.7 million ounces used in October–December, 1972.

This news was even more bullish than anyone expected, and the market reacted to it like any self-respecting bull market should. On the next trading day, Tuesday, May 29 (Monday being a holiday), New York silver warehouse stocks were down 330,000 ounces and the market was up the limit. (Figure 17.)

I'm now projecting a near-term price objective of 275.00–280.00 for July, with a longer-term objective of 340.00–360.00 for more distant futures. This silver market looks like a repeat of our recent Copper Caper; we just have to stay patient and relaxed. Remember, the big money is made sitting—not trading, just sitting. I keep hearing Dr. G's amused comments about our "baby bulls," and how they keep getting snookered out of their long positions.

Our silver adventure will be concluded in Chapter 18.

"Let's Just Do One Contract—
How Much Can We Lose?"

11

Every once in a while some young innocent hits me with that line. You know, the "What the hell, how much can we lose?" trade. And my response: "Pick a number. Make it a *very big* number. *That's* how much you can lose on one contract."

And who do you suppose is prime candidate No. 1 for this sermon? Me, that's who.

I've been trading soybeans since 1960, and it's always been one of my favorite markets, what with big volume, broad price swings, excellent trend characteristics, and plenty of good catchable action. As a matter of fact, my first major commodity involvement was during the big 1961 soybean bull market.

And even in 1972 I "caught" the bean market twice. I bought May bean oil around 10.30¢ and sold it, just a few weeks later, at 11.30¢. (It subsequently scampered up to 17.00¢, much to my surprise.) And remember my soybean "coup" described in Chapter 2? That was where I bought May beans at 3.19, more at 3.22, and even paid "as high as" 3.24, ultimately selling out the entire position at 3.36—just before the bean market commenced its record-shattering price advance.

So when soybeans attained the ridiculous, unsustainable, unheard-of price of 8.58, on May 21, I just "knew" they were a short sale. The market had exceeded its maximum upside count, all

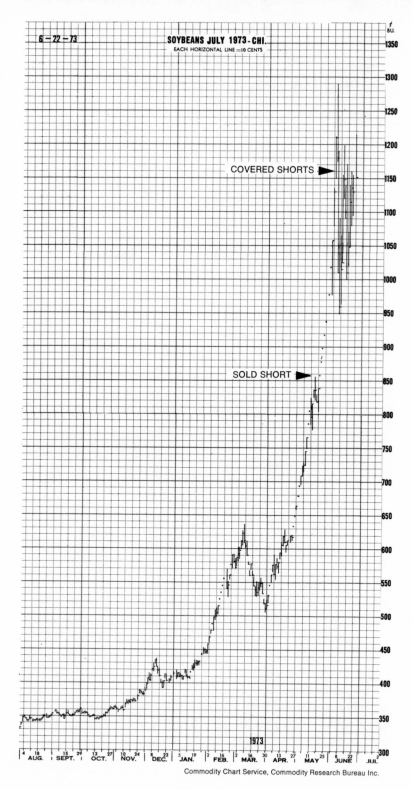

Figure 18.

technical indicators said "overbought," and past bean bull markets had generally topped out during May or June. But, being always the careful, prudent speculator, and knowing that I was selling against both the major and the minor trends (that was O.K., I rationalized; the market was "about to" collapse), I decided to take just a small short position. My plan was to "pile on" after the trend had turned down and my shorts were in the money. (At least I did *something* right!)

So I put out a small line of shorts in July beans around the 8.58 level, seemingly a relatively safe level to be short. And I resolved that if I was wrong (and the market would tell me soon enough), I wouldn't overstay—I'd just get out and take the loss.

And that's exactly what I did, since the market told me, in no uncertain terms, that I was wrong. I covered the short position just two weeks later, on June 4, for a *loss of $15,930 per contract.*

Aside from losing money, this soybean debacle hurt me in another way. During the period that I was struggling with beans, the rest of my trading suffered badly, and that really hurt. Sitting with even a small losing position relative to other much larger winning positions can do that to a trader. Losses are inevitable—and although I'm adjusted to accepting losses, fortunately not losses of that magnitude, I'm also accustomed to being able to ferret out and get aboard winning commodity positions, adding to my line as the market moves favorably, and eventually scoring big profits. (Figure 18.)

However, notwithstanding that I had just taken $1.2 million out of copper and that I was currently sitting long some 200 silver contracts with big profits at the beginning of a major bull market, my modest 25-contract short soybean position really bugged and unnerved me. So much so that I chickened out of taking two market positions for which I had been patiently waiting: I canceled large orders to buy September corn on a buy stop at 1.80 (it ultimately moved up to 3.47), and to buy December copper in the 64.00–65.00¢ range (it subsequently exceeded 100.00¢).

It just goes to prove, once again, that no market is ever too high to buy, or too low to sell. In retrospect soybeans were still a good buy at 8.58. They still had another 4.00 left on the upside—equal to $20,000 per contract. And brother, that's not hay!

What's More Important Than Knowing WHEN to Trade?

12

Several years ago, while driving along the New Jersey Turnpike from New York to Philadelphia, I had an uneasy feeling. The traffic was moving along a little too fast; the road was a little too slippery; the few turns and twists seemed more dangerous than usual. The limited visibility seemed to confuse many motorists, so that they appeared to be operating with reckless abandon. And I observed more than the usual number of accidents alongside the road, with people injured, or even worse—all of which created more difficulties and confusion for the other motorists. My senses blinked CAUTION . . . CAUTION . . . CAUTION—and I pulled off the road to sit on the sidelines until conditions seemed more suitable for the safe and successful continuance of my journey.

I experienced the same uneasy feeling about many of the commodity markets during mid-1973. My impression was that everything was exceptionally high: *high* prices, *high* volume, *high* open interest, and *high* risk—*excessively high risk.*

That was the year in which the large NYSE wire houses "discovered" the commodity markets. In doing so, they learned not only that a commodity trader generates more gross commissions than a stock trader with a given-size margin account but also that a given gross commission in a commodity trade will result in a ·

much higher net profit return than the same size of commission in a stock trade. The commodity exchanges realized this, too, and encouraged stockbrokerage firms to major in commodity trading with the type of advertising shown in Figure 19:

Where have all the individual investors gone?

Take a look at Chicago Mercantile Exchange volume. Every year, more and more brokers are recommending CME commodity trading to selected customers.

That's understandable. Wouldn't you like to have more customers who trade 40 or 50 times a year?

Interested?   Send the coupon.

CHICAGO MERCANTILE EXCHANGE
444 West Jackson Blvd., Chicago, Illinois 60606

Gentlemen: Dept. 546
   Please send me your current information for brokers.

NAME _____

FIRM _____

ADDRESS _____

CITY _____ STATE _____ ZIP _____

Figure 19.

And it succeeded, for, as reported by *Barron's* of January 29, 1973 "Commodities are the newest game in town, so statistics and the launching of commodity departments by Wall Street firms alike suggest."

What's good for a Wall Street commission firm isn't, however, necessarily good for the individual speculator—particularly one who's more interested in profits than in new games. No wonder my mind started churning with "highway" disaster thoughts:

And how they did "enjoy" it. The *Wall Street Journal*, on July 7, 1973, reported: "A second British company this week has found that cocoa isn't its cup of tea." During a single week, two large British firms, William Baird & Co. and Rowntree Macintosh, Ltd., reported losses of $3.8 and $50 million respectively (the $50-million loss was subsequently "revalued" up to $78 million), as a result of losing transactions in cocoa futures. As Rowntree's deputy chairman explained the loss: "The dealer got carried away. . . . A man can develop an absolute conviction that his view of future price trends is correct, even though the market as a whole is moving the other way." A sporting attitude, I'd say. They should have read Chapter 4.

Meanwhile, back in New York, Wall Street watchers noted that among the many securities firms that folded during 1973 were two old-line investment houses that merged involuntarily with

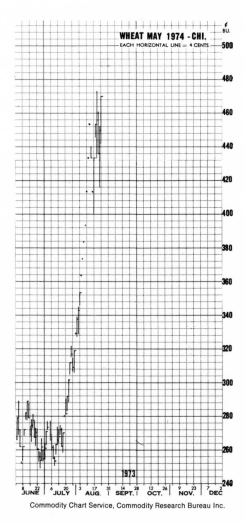

Commodity Chart Service, Commodity Research Bureau Inc.

Figure 20.

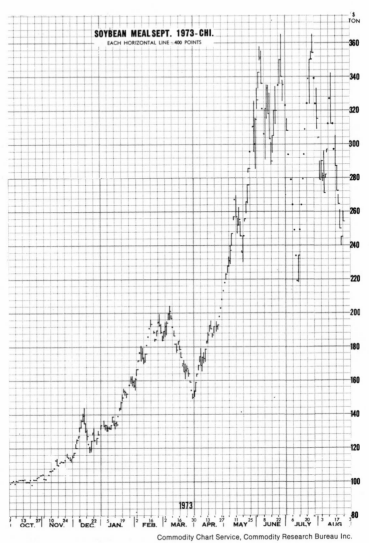

Figure 21.

The dots on the price charts represent limit moves, with few or no trades executed on the respective days.

other firms. Interestingly, although both these firms' commodity business was essentially a minor part of their overall operation, their demise was due directly to commodity miscalculations. Their customers were trapped in short soybean positions during the late great bull market, and couldn't (or wouldn't) come up with the variation margin to cover several successive limit advances. So the firms had to post all that margin themselves—and they just ran out of money.

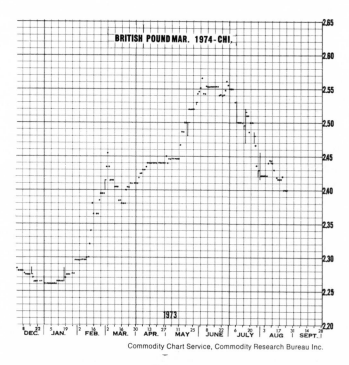

Commodity Chart Service, Commodity Research Bureau Inc.

Figure 22.

There were many other disastrous instances like these. If such experienced, well-capitalized professional firms did so poorly, one wonders how the vast body of "amateur" speculators made out during this period.

On June 1, 1973, the prestigious Commodity Research Bureau had this to say about the state of the market:

Futures markets appear to be gripped by a kind of mob hysteria and panic buying in recent weeks has resulted. The venerable Chicago

Board of Trade held a series of emergency meetings in an attempt to keep the markets viable in the face of unprecedented "limit" advances. With the CRB Index tacking on another huge gain and gold prices soaring to new record highs, we were prompted to re-read the famous classic *Extraordinary Popular Delusions and the Madness of Crowds* by Mackay. Current market action, in our opinion, is in the tradition of famous economic madnesses such as "The Mississippi Delusion" and "The Tulip Bulb Craze." Because crowd action is irrational, there is no telling when crowd love will turn to hate. To paraphrase a famous Bernard Baruch quote about keeping one's sense of balance: "Even in the very presence of dizzily spiraling prices, we should all continuously repeat, two and two still make four."

My resolve to stay in a predominantly cash position in mid-1973 was strengthened every time I looked at the commodity price charts. Charts 20 to 22, typical of many markets during this period, demonstrate the difficulty and frustration of trading these markets successfully.

What do some of the Street's most successful professionals say about operating during such wild, unpredictable markets?

RW: Take lots of long vacations.

JM: Don't play if the game is too wild. If you trip along the way, OK to sprain your ankle—just don't get your neck broken. That way you're out of the game permanently.

A leading commodity firm's market letter[*] summarized the situation:

> Numerous limit-up days have been seen . . . with little in the way of any significant reaction indicating that the speculative bubble may be in the last and sharpest wave up. When this bubble bursts it will come when all persons are fully bullish and, therefore, fully committed to the long side psychologically and vulnerable to a sharp and heavy downmove. When—soon, but we don't know exactly. How —more than likely due to an overbought excessiveness and not necessarily any government intervention. We suggest reading the book *Extraordinary Popular Delusions and the Madness of Crowds,* to see how the tulip mania of early Holland ended; essentially it was overnight.

Kroll's advice is more succinct: WHEN IN DOUBT, STAY OUT.

[*] ACLI-Dreyfus & Co., Chicago.

A Modest Proposal:
"Buy Us Two Thousand Platinums"

13

Wednesday, 8:30 A.M., February 14, 1973: I watched the silent orange lights above the elevator door call off the floors—32 . . . 33 . . . 34 . . . the car was slowing down . . . 35 . . . 36 . . . and the paneled doors slid open. Quietly, cautiously, I got off. Seated at a large steel desk, perhaps 30 feet back in the starkly modern antechamber, was a blue-uniformed receptionist. He watched me intently as I approached. Before I had covered half the distance to him he had fingered a combination of buttons on a side console. Almost instantly, two blue lights flashed on his panel. He motioned me to a massive blue Mies Barcelona chair at one end of the room.

What is this whole crazy thing about, I kept asking myself. I'd been in suspense since Monday evening, two days earlier, when I got the telephone call. It was an overseas call, from Albert, a banker with whom I had conducted certain business dealings last year. He was brief and to the point, just as I had remembered him. Two of his associates would meet me, to discuss "certain matters," at 8:30 A.M. on Wednesday, at an address I recognized immediately. That's all there was to the conversation. I remember thinking that at 9:00 P.M. in New York it was 2:00 A.M. in Europe. Albert was not exactly known as a night owl; it must have been something pretty important to keep him up that late.

"O.K.," I said, "I'll be there."

I barely had time to clear my throat properly—I always do that when I'm nervous—when a sneaky little door slid open on the other side of the room, and my taciturn friend in blue motioned me through.

It was a long corridor, perhaps six feet wide, thickly carpeted and brightly fluorescented. There was one open door at the end of the corridor, which I gauged to be my destination. It was.

Seated at a massive circular teak and rosewood conference table were Albert's two "associates," Dr. P and Mr. G. Dr. P got right to the point. "Mr. Kroll, do you know what this is?" he asked, extending a small object in his right hand. "My associates [or did he say accomplices?] and I want to buy 2,000 contracts of platinum on the Exchange." And he fell silent.

My turn. "Look," I said, "that's terrific. But why all the cloak-and-dagger stuff? Just pick up your phone, call Merrill Lynch, and tell them you want to buy some platinum. They'll be glad to do it for you." My turn to be silent now.

Dr. P leaned forward and cleared his throat. (So, he was nervous, too.) "But, you see, Mr. Kroll, we want to buy the entire position for under $150, basis the January future."

SK: (So that's the game. January should be around $164.00 today, and the market's strong. His 2,000-contract buying order could easily run prices up to $180.00.)

Dr. P: Can you do it?

SK: How much money do you have?

Dr. P: How much will you need?

SK: (He must be kidding.) You're joking, aren't you?

Dr. P: Am I?

SK: (He's not joking!)
(A long pause.)

Dr. P: Well, can you do it?

This time we all cleared our throats.

Getting down to the nitty-gritty:

SK: O.K., O.K., I'm in. Four million ought to handle it—but just to play it safe, let's make it eight million. The extra four million will be our insurance. We'll put six million into Treasuries—can use them for original margin—and two million in cash ought to be plenty for any maintenance calls.

Dr. P: Fine. How do you propose to run the orders?

SK: I've already got direct lines to my brokers on the floor. I'll put lines into three of the major wire houses and two large trade houses. Do you have any companies we can use up front? Preferably with Exchange memberships—no point in losing all that brokerage.

Mr. G: We'll be able to provide you with the necessary accommodations.

SK: Fine. You'll brief me on that later today, say around noon. Now about the money—where will it be and when will it be there?

Dr. P: We'll be using these three banks (and he handed me a small card with three names typed on it). The necessary funds will be at your disposal by 1:00 P.M. today, well before the market closes.

SK: By the way, is Albert in on this deal, and may I check it out with him this evening?

Dr. P: Your answer is yes to both questions.

SK: (He sure doesn't waste any words.) Good. We'll get started this morning. Gold fixed at 70.10 and 72.30 in London, and with silver up 1.10 pence, I'm looking for New York platinum to open perhaps 300 higher than last night's close. We couldn't buy in any size without really marking prices up, and handing over a huge windfall to the specs who're sitting on the long side.

Mr. G: You are suggesting that the market is presently too crowded for your liking, no?

SK: Yes, yes, of course. Volume has been running around 500 lots daily, with open interest under 7,000. Let's speed up the pace now—really get it hopping—and start moving prices around. You'll be seeing volume over 1,000 daily for the next month or so, with open interest going over 8,000. If we are serious about accumulating a line of Januarys under 150.00, we'll have to see the market up first—really high. I want to see plenty of bullish stories being circulated, with a couple of thousand new longs coming in at high prices—say over 175.00, maybe as high as 190.00 to 200.00. We'll paint a bullish chart for the boys, replete with timely bullish news releases—that auto-exhaust catalyst story is always good for a quick 400 or 500 points if the market is technically ready for an advance. And I suppose we can shake out some commission-house buy recommendations at crucial points. We'll see the market so overbought that when it finally drops, it'll be like wet garbage pouring out the bottom of a soggy paper bag—kabloosh!

Mr. G: And then we buy, no?

SK: And then we buy, yes. But you have something against helping the market along here and there—you know, sort of massaging it up and down a bit?

(Dr. P leaned back in his chair and smiled. He knew. I could learn to like him, I thought to myself. Dr. P kept on smiling while I told him what my share of the operation would be. Good man, I thought—he didn't even flinch.)

SK: My share is simple. I take half of the total commission that we save by trading at member rates, plus 15 percent of the net profit of the entire operation. (This could reach $300,000, I reckoned—not bad for "painting" chart pictures.)

My new "partners" both smiled this time. No one had cleared his throat for the past half hour—a good sign. They reached across the table and shook my hand. Done!

Postscript

Well, now that I've told the story, I'll say one more thing about it: it didn't really happen—at least not to my knowledge.

So, please excuse me for this little fictional episode—the only piece of fiction in the book. I did it, first of all, because I enjoyed concocting the story. But mostly because I thought you might enjoy seeing how a commodity market *could be* manipulated—and see how neatly this fictional episode fits in with what actually did happen in the market, as described in the following chapter.

The Platinum Kid Scores (???)

14

At the end of Chapter 8 the Platinum Kid, tenuously hanging onto 200 long platinum contracts, was seen doing a rally dance, invoking an advance above 166.00 (basis July) so that he could buy another 100 lots on the subsequent reaction to the 154.00 area. Although I'm never certain of a rally in platinum, I can always count on a sharp, swift reaction following an advance. Whenever the big commission houses get bullish on platinum and are heavy buyers for customers' accounts, one of those "little" shakeouts happens to come along—and they can be murder!

The rally dance must have worked, because in the 3 weeks between February 12 and March 2, platinum moved onward and upward, absolutely astonishing even the most bullish platinum watchers. A 4,400-point move (equal to $2,200 per 50-ounce contract) in just three weeks. And on heavy volume—over 1,000 contracts daily, and a big expansion in open interest—it reached 8,700 contracts. It seemed to me unreal, as though some powerful interest was determined to move the market up. But who could have wanted the platinum that badly, at those high prices? There was no apparent logic to it.

On Friday, March 2, the market opened on a huge upward gap, some 800 points higher (July opened at 186.00), largely on the strength of a major wire house's buy flash and its heavy buying, at the market, on the opening call. This, too, was totally illogical. Platinum had just advanced some $40 per ounce in just six weeks, and *now* they were loading up their customers on the long side. Why?

Would July reach my 195.00 price objective on this surge? I could hardly believe the strength of this market, fueled by a wild speculative buying spree, and I was ready to sell out my entire 200-contract position around the 190.00 level. What happened next? I'll spare you the suspense. Of course, the market fell just short of my sell price. Values weakened throughout the session, with the market closing on the day's lows. Here was a classic reversal day: heavy volume, the market opening on a huge gap at new life-of-contract highs, and closing on the day's low, below the previous close. Well, here comes the reaction, I figured. Perhaps even a big shake-out, but it's still a bull market. Only the minor trend turned down, the major trend is still up—so I'll just sit tight and not lose my position. After all, didn't I anticipate this type of action? Remember, on any close above 166.00 (basis July), expect a reaction, and wait to rebuy another 100 lots on that reaction. So here was that reaction.

I was anticipating a decline down to around 154.00 to 156.00. The market should find good buying support at that level, which coincided with a 50 percent retracement of the recent 136.00 to 186.00 advance.

While the market was declining, I held my ground and waited patiently to buy more. I kept thinking of Jesse Livermore's advice:

> I have learned . . . to take a position and stick to it. I can wait without a twinge of impatience. I can see a setback without being shaken, knowing that it is only temporary. I have been short 100,000 shares and I have seen a big rally coming. I have figured—and figured correctly—that such a rally as I felt was inevitable, and even wholesome, would make a difference of one million dollars in my paper profits. And I nevertheless have stood pat and seen half my paper profit wiped out, without once considering the advisability of covering my shorts to put them out again on the rally. I knew that if I did I might lose my position and with it the certainty of a big killing. It is the big swing that makes the big money for you.

Well, on Friday, March 9, July platinum opened at 157.00 and worked lower throughout the session, closing at 149.60. In accordance with my game plan (detailed in Chapter 8), I bought another 100 Octobers on that setback. I wasn't buying any more Julys—didn't want to get too heavy in the soon-to-expire July contract. My anticipated support around the 154.00 level didn't materialize, and I watched in anguish as the market tumbled another 1,500 points, to around 140.00 (basis July), before encountering substantial buying interest.

The next 6 weeks were tense for me—sitting in this "dumb" market, long 300 contracts—as values fluctuated within a trading range from 140.00 to 150.00. Volume diminished, averaging perhaps 500 lots daily, and the public commission-house speculator demonstrated, once again, his unerring and recurring penchant for being on the losing side of the market. Where he was wildly bullish above 170.00, he had turned discouraged and bearish below 145.00. It was obvious that the public speculators were selling out long positions, *on the reactions;* the total open interest had declined from 8,700 to 6,300 contracts between March 2 and May 4.

But it was becoming very obvious that there were more than just the "baby bulls and bears" in this market. There appeared to be major interests present who, although unseen, left their fingerprints in other ways. Someone was handing out contracts around the 150.00 level, and he seemingly had unlimited funds with which to back up his market view; on the other hand, he was just as consistently buying contracts, probably covering shorts as well, around the 140.00 level.

Some 15,000 platinum contracts changed hands during this six-week period—twice the total number of contracts in the entire market. Was it just my imagination that the long side was inexorably and silently shifting from weak to strong hands? But why? Who were the buyers, and why were they supporting the market so tenaciously?

Who cared *why!* My observation and instinct told me that there was a large-scale, major accumulation going on. Let the theorists and analysts ponder over *why* it was happening. It sufficed for me to know that *it was happening.* Period!

So, I just hung in there, plenty nervous to be sure, but I knew that I was right. With this major buying interest in the market—around the 140.00 level for July, coinciding with 144.00 for

October and 148.00 for January—I felt that sooner or later the supply of contracts offered for sale at these levels would dry up. The sellers would capitulate, and the market would embark on the next stage of the accumulation—the "marking up" (price advance) stage.

The 140.00 to 150.00 six-week trading range was broken on April 16, as July traded down to 136.00, remained there for all of two days, and then started moving up again. This looked like classic bottoming action, with professional traders pressing the market down to touch off whatever stops (stop-loss orders to sell) may be "resting" below the market. They didn't find much—total volume for the two days came to just 1,050 contracts, further supporting my view that the market was extremely oversold and was ready for a recovery. But to what level? (Figure 23.)

We were now sitting long 300 contracts, which was too heavy a position for such a thin market, subject to seemingly unpredictable, irrational fluctuations. Perhaps too unpredictable, too irrational. This market wasn't for me, and I decided to start moving out. The big question was: where and how to sell?

Well, since the market couldn't make any headway on the break below 140.00, my instincts told me that the next surge would be through the 150.00 resistance level. Such a rally would catch a lot of traders by surprise, and should generate enough buying momentum to rally prices some 50 percent of the previous 186.00 to 136.00 down leg—or back to about 160.00 (July). Major resistance should enter the market around 165.00, for July, and I'd be contributing to that selling pressure.

The market was wild, but it generally followed that script. July rallied to 160.00, retreated to 149.00, back up to 161.00, down to 146.00, all the way back up to 168.00, and then right down to 146.00. Get the picture? (See Figure 23.)

During the week of June 4, I sold my Julys above the 160.00 level. With my platinum position considerably lightened, I was now able to sit back and look for better opportunities to close out the remaining October positions. In effect, I had "sold down to a sleeping level," and I was able to take a more relaxed view and let the market come to me. And it did. But I also had other market forces on my side—the other precious metals were strong, and that strength was spilling over into the platinum market. Silver, for

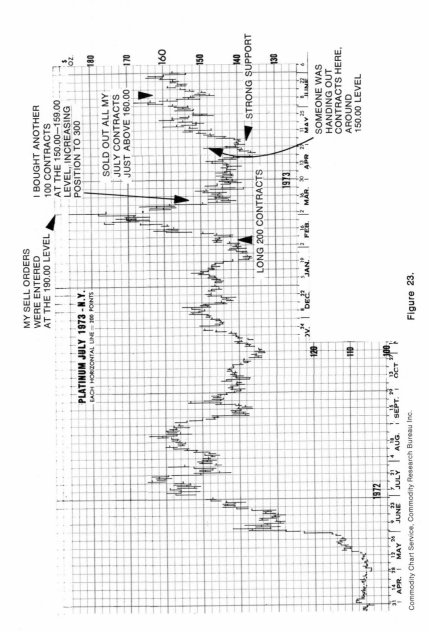

Figure 23.

Commodity Chart Service, Commodity Research Bureau Inc.

example, was experiencing a 60¢ advance, with gold advancing some $30 per ounce.

As the platinum market rallied, I began to have second thoughts about selling out. Should I cancel the sell orders and sit? Maybe even buy some more? Hell, no! Enough of that nonsense! Here I was, starting to get bullish again just because the market was moving up. Stay strong, Kroll, stick to the original premise— it still makes good sense. So I managed to get some of the Octobers off around 180.00, but I probably averaged 170.00 to 175.00 on the overall position.

Not as big a score as I would have expected, and I was a little disappointed, because I had agonized over that position. But I was glad to be out of it, and I breathed a long sigh of relief when the final sell orders got off. Oh, I also took a couple of days off and went sailing—figured I had earned the rest.

The Broker "Tells" You—
but Who "Tells" the Broker?

15

"Mr. Winston, our research department has just issued a bullish flash on bellies. Thought you might like to take five Febs at the market."

"Your short silver position looks vulnerable, Mrs. Parker. I'd suggest you enter a protective stop order, or else cover the Marches right here."

"I don't see anything to do in the market, Mr. Larkin, but some of the other brokers here are going into soybeans, and it might be right up your alley."

"Look, Tom, if you can't come up with the margin check, you'd better sell out the position on the close. Otherwise they're going to sell you out at the opening tomorrow."

Sure, you've all heard that sort of advice from your brokers. But, to whom do the brokers go when they need advice on how to run their commodity business? Well, sometimes they come to me.

With the commodity markets really burning up the track, in the face of a listless and generally unprofitable stock market, the attention of Wall Street's securities firms has been increasingly turning toward commodities. But Wall Street pros move slowly. They've been burned too many times in the past, jumping prematurely into new ventures.

Thus, when I was asked by the Investment Association of New

York, a group of some 600 of the Street's younger executives, to speak at their 1973 fall lecture series, I was given the general topic, "What Should Wall Street Do About Commodities, and How?"

Here are the pertinent sections of my speech, "Silver Threads Among the Pork Bellies, or, Wall Street Discovers Commodities."

Why should a Wall Street investment firm want to get into the commodity trading business? The most obvious reason would be to make money. There is much more commission income to be made through commodity brokerage, relatively speaking, than through stock or bond brokerage. Let's take a look at a few reasons why Wall Streeters are intrigued at the profit potential of commodity brokerage:

Activity is concentrated in just a few dozen markets and trading turnover is much greater than in stocks.

There are invariably much higher gross commissions on a commodity trading account than on the same size of stock account. It is not unusual for an active commodity trader to rack up gross commissions equal to his entire trading capital in as little as a year's time. In a study conducted by researchers at the University of Illinois of futures trading at a major commission firm during 1970–71, for example, it was noted that the firm's customers showed a *gross* profit of $2.6 million. However, commissions amounted to $8.0 million, so there was actually a *net trading loss* of $5.4 million. I would, of course, prefer to see the mathematics more favorable to the customers.

Commodity back-office work is considerably simpler and less involved than it is for stocks. It is estimated that there are 66 individual steps in the processing of a stock transaction; there are no more than 12 to 14 in the typical commodity transaction. Thus, commodity commission business is significantly cheaper to handle, resulting in a much higher takedown to net.

And finally, the public is intrigued with commodity trading, so that it's much easier to get a trader to move into commodities than into stocks. If you have any doubts about it, just consider this: A commodity trader can buy or sell a contract of silver, worth over $50,000, by posting $5,000 in margin and paying a round-turn commission, covering both the purchase and the sale, for just

$45.50. And if he makes it a day trade, the total commission is just $23. Compare this sort of arithmetic with a person buying or selling 200 shares of a $250 stock—his margin is $25,000, and the round-turn commission on the transaction is $300, with no reduction for a day trade.

Whether a brokerage firm wishes to attract a wide cross section of commodity clients or wishes to specialize in serving just speculators, hedgers, or tax straddlers depends on how the firm weighs the various risk/reward factors of each aspect of the business. As in all businesses, commodity brokerage has its positive and negative factors, and so do each of the three different types of brokerage business. Which of the following clients would you like to deal with, given the corresponding plus and minus factors?

Speculators

Plus side: This is the easiest kind of business to get, and it shows both the highest rate of commission and client turnover. Moreover, speculators are usually nonmember traders, so the business is done at full commission rates.

Also, the firm can generate additional income by putting its clients' excess nonregulated funds into Treasuries; and on some exchanges it can even post these Treasuries as original margin.

Minus side: If the commodity trading goes poorly, the firm could lose a good stock account. I remember, in 1963, when one of the largest stock customers at a firm I was with decided to dabble in sugar. He actually made a small overall profit on his sugar dealings, but was advised to close out a long position two days before the market really exploded on the upside. I never saw a more infuriated customer—he just couldn't be placated, and he pulled his substantial securities portfolio out of the firm.

Furthermore, if a commodity account goes into deficit (and in these volatile markets it could easily happen), the firm is responsible to the clearinghouse whether or not the client pays. As a matter of fact, several NYSE firms, including some of the largest, are reputed to have suffered substantial losses in 1973 because their clients were short on soybeans while the market experienced 12 consecutive limit-up sessions.

Trade Hedgers

Plus side: Clients are more likely to be experienced, well capitalized, and more responsible than the average speculator. The commission firm will probably have less responsibility for trading decisions, and has less chance of getting stuck for deficit accounts. A good trade hedger knows his soybeans from his potatoes better than most stockholders know General Motors from Ford.

Minus side: It is more difficult to get these clients, since there are fewer prospects, and nearly all the commodity firms go after them.

Many trade hedgers are companies which are also exchange members, so they trade on half rates of commission. Also, some exchanges permit brokers to extend credit to trade hedgers, so a commission firm must maintain higher capital in order to engage safely in this type of business.

Tax Straddlers

Plus factors: Since the client is usually simultaneously long and short, the broker can structure the positions so that there will be less risk to both the client and the firm. Naturally, there's a knack to doing this. In addition, commission charges in most tax-straddle transactions run quite high.

Minus factors: Margins are low and the positions are large, so the positions must be carefully researched before being recommended and must be closely watched.

Also, there's the risk that an overzealous salesman might inadvertently give tax advice to a client, which could subsequently backfire. I suggest that the firm assign certain experienced men to handle the tax-straddle business for its clients, and that all dealings be done in conjunction with the client's tax counsel.

Well, let's say by now you're itching to get into the commodity business. You've weighed the plus and minus factors; you're amply capitalized, and you've got a couple of hot-shot account executives who are really enthusiastic about becoming commodity brokers.

And several of your better-heeled clients have been starting to inquire about commodity trading.

Just how do you go about expanding your firm into the commodity business? If it requires such minimal back-office work, and relatively low overhead, with the customers just clamoring for commodity services, then you would think that setting up a department would be a relatively simple matter, right?

Wrong.

Before you go out and join commodity exchanges, lease a commodity board, and start training personnel, ask yourself a few simple questions:

1. What is the firm's real motivation? If it's just a short-range interest to cash in on a currently hot piece of business, without a full commitment to do it properly, forget it. You'll be out on the street selling another commodity—apples—before you realize it.

2. The firm must study and understand the business, set realistic goals and objectives, and make the necessary commitments in terms of capital, personnel, research, and facilities.

Specifically, the firm must consider:

a. What sort of business it does at present. If you're research- or wholesale-oriented, it may not be realistic to attempt a general commission business; you might be better advised pursuing trade hedging or tax-straddle business, neither of which requires much of a retail sales staff. If you're retail-oriented, are your clients predominantly large or small traders, speculative or conservative?

b. Does it have knowledgeable, committed, and experienced full-time management to oversee the commodity operation? You can't sell raincoats if all you know is tractors. In 1963, I was meeting with the senior partner of a large NYSE member firm, applying for a position as manager of their rather sizable commodity department. I wasn't hired because, as the senior partner told me, "we already have a commodity department manager." He then introduced me to his "manager," a young man who spent most of his day on the exchange floor with the senior partner, his uncle, who came back to the office every day, at three o'clock, to "manage" the commodity department. Perhaps I was less surprised than most Wall Street watchers when the firm went broke as a result of massive commodity problems.

c. The existing research philosophy of the firm—is it compatible with the approach to be taken in commodities?

Here are the prerequisites for setting up a fully competent commodity department:

a. *Regulatory requirements* dictate that the firm must register annually with the Commodity Exchange Authority (CEA) as a so-called Futures Commission Merchant, at an annual cost of $200 plus $6 for each branch office. Obtain a copy of the CEA regulations and study them carefully. They call for very special segregated handling of customers' regulated funds, and there are strict penalties for noncompliance. There have been several cases of large brokerage firms' being censured by the CEA for rule infractions that apparently were the result of nothing more than bookkeeping oversights. The procedure for handling, segregating, and accounting for customers' regulated funds must be vigilantly watched.

b. Regarding *exchange memberships,* there are three ways a firm can conduct its commodity business:

1. As a *nonmember,* in which case it retains no part of the commissions. Obviously, this is not the way to go.

2. As a *nonclearing exchange member.* The firm retains half the commission, with the clearing firm keeping the other half.

3. As a full *clearing firm.* The firm retains the full commission, less the floor brokerage and a small clearance fee.

The following table illustrates the above discussion:*

	Pays	Bellies	Silver	Soy Beans
Nonmember	full commission	$46.50	$45.50	$30.00
Member (nonclearing)	half commission	$23.00	$23.00	$15.00
Clearing Member	floor brokerage plus clearance fee	$ 3.50	$ 5.50	$ 3.50

Commodity brokers can operate either on a disclosed basis, giving up their customers, by name, to another carrying broker, or on an omnibus account basis. This is similar to the arrangements for carrying securities accounts.

* Figures as of February 1974.

Commodity-exchange seats are purchased by individuals; the firms do not buy seats. After becoming a member, an individual may apply for his firm to be accorded membership trading privileges, but the seat holder must be either a general partner or a voting stockholder of the firm. Prices of seats vary, from around $11,000 for the New York Mercantile Exchange to around $105,000 for the Chicago Mercantile Exchange.

Start trading modestly at first. You might even consider trading through some other clearing firm, on a fully disclosed basis, until your firm has obtained sufficient experience. In such a situation, the introducing broker is usually responsible for original margin, while the carrying broker would be responsible for maintenance (variation) margin. When you think your firm is ready, the accounts can be switched to an omnibus basis, and you can start doing your own bookkeeping.

Now, what about physical facilities and personnel?

Order clerks must be trained, but your clearing firm should be able to train your present clerks. Entering commodity orders isn't greatly different from stock orders, but speed and accuracy—above all, accuracy—are vital.

If you are properly automated—and there are some experienced service-bureau firms that can automate your entire back-office operation economically—two or three clerks in your operations department can efficiently handle a substantial volume of business. Here again, your clearing firm will help you set it up.

However, the ingredient that is most vitally required is *management,* whose responsibilities include:

1. Organizing and operating the business on a sound, safe, and profitable basis.

2. Constantly supervising and upgrading the operation.

3. Not trying to cut corners regarding personnel. You'll need the best people you can find.

Let's focus, for a moment, on formulating a business concept and adhering to it. You must consider:

1. What type of business to go after.

2. Who will solicit commodity business—all salesmen, or just certain specified people?

3. Which customers to approach, and how.

4. The possibility of handling discretionary accounts and employee commodity trading. I would say no to both, at least in the beginning of the operation.

On another level, don't be greedy for business. It's frequently more important to know when to say no than yes. For example, in mid-1970 a big trader came to my office to open an account. He would trade completely on his own, he said. I felt uneasy about him and was reluctant to accept the account. Then he started bragging about how big a trader he was: "I trade 200-contract positions, and you'll get plenty of commissions from my account." That settled it for me; I turned him down. When he asked why, I said: "I can handle a 20-contract mistake, but a 200-contract mistake—that could put me out of business." I was glad I said no. I know of some good-size commodity firms that were put out of business because of the "mistakes" of just one large freewheeling customer.

Finally, you should know how to promote and expand your commodity business.

First of all, don't try to grow too fast. Plan your expansion in an orderly manner and be sure that your sales force isn't getting too big for either your capital position or your back-office capability.

Before you worry about how to attract new clients, be sure that you are doing the right things to keep your existing clients happy.

If you do advertise or give lectures, first study what everyone else is doing and make a judgment on what seems to be working best. Then when you do promote, stress your strong points. You may have an excellent precious-metals analyst and do particularly well in that area, then that's the area to stress.

Just remember: Operating a commodity business is a lot like trading in commodities. You have the potential for making really big money—or losing it if you're not on the ball.

As the reader may gather from the above excerpted talk, there isn't a great difference in approaching the commodity business from the customer's or the broker's point of view.

Yet, what I've presented is not only a little peek into what the

Street says to itself about wise commodity trading but also what a potential speculator should know when approaching a brokerage firm.

Here's a suggestion to the commodity neophyte, or to the experienced trader who feels that he isn't getting all the service he should have: reread this chapter sometime, and run down the list of suggestions I made to the brokerage representatives. Then pick out the points you feel are most important to you, and write them down in the form of questions.

When you're ready to take your account to a brokerage firm, or when you're considering pulling out of one firm and going with another, ask those questions—and expect some straight answers from all concerned.

Your final question, of course, should be: "What has your trading record been over the past few years?" Don't be satisfied with being shown market letters and paper trading figures; ask to see some actual profit-and-loss summaries from customers' accounts. Most firms will immediately protest that this would be unethical disclosure (coincidentally, most firms' customers lose money). But if they simply delete all references to the customers' identities and only show you the figures, there's nothing unethical about that. If they've made money, they'll show you the figures. If they haven't, they'll either get huffy or try to dissuade you. You be the judge!

Tiptoe into My Office and Be a Fly on the Wall

16

MR. STANLEY KROLL

REQUESTS THE PLEASURE OF YOUR COMPANY

ON HIS OFFICE WALL

OCTOBER THROUGH NOVEMBER, 1973

25 BROAD STREET, SUITE 643

NEW YORK CITY

Since 1964 my base of operations has been a suite of offices on the sixth floor of 25 Broad Street, one of Wall Street's grand, traditional office towers. My desk is ensconced within a carpeted, walnut-furnished, glass-walled room of 10 by 20 feet, overlooking my main board room with its adjacent charting room, conference room, and two back-office rooms. We pay rent on 2,100 square feet of floor space, although I sometimes suspect that that figure includes the thickness of the building's massive brick-and-stone exterior walls.

My office staff numbers three, and our entire bookkeeping and back-office functions are completely automated. Each evening we send to our data-processing center, by messenger, trade tickets and sheets noting the day's journal and bookkeeping entries. During the night, these data are punched onto IBM cards, fed into the computer, and presto . . . out pop the various trade confirmations, P & S slips, debit and credit advices, and an entire updated account "run" covering all commodity positions, equities, debits and credits, and other financial summaries. Even our general ledger.

During the working day, the office is a quiet, restful haven within a noisy, frenzied community. Friends of mine from the brokerage or banking fraternity are forever popping in. I used to inquire why they came up, but the reply usually went something like this: "to sit down quietly and collect my thoughts for a while." So I don't even ask any more.

I can be found daily, jacketless and frequently shoeless, doing my thing: trading in the market to try to make money, lots of money. How do I do it? Specifically, what do I do all day, day after day, in pursuing my thing?

Well, I've got this idea: why don't you

tiptoe into my office and be a *quiet* fly on the wall?

You're invited!

Thursday, October 25, 1973

Today was one of those wild, irrational trading days typical of some we've had recently. I spent the morning in Washington, but before I left New York I checked the opening indications for the markets. We were expecting higher prices all over the board. Well, the markets did open strong—silver up 300 points, soybeans up 15¢, and corn 7¢ higher. Some strong opening! But when I returned to the office, around 1:30, the prices had abruptly turned around and were making new lows. Beans were down 7¢, silver had plummeted 500 points, and corn had slipped 3¢. Just as I was surveying the damage, everything firmed up again and . . . away we go! On the close, soybeans were plus 7¢, corn was up 5¢, and silver had firmed a bit, down only 150 points (after a day like this, that's almost like being ahead!).

The really bright spot was plywood, which was up the limit (700 points). I had been thinking of selling the plywood position, but after such a strong limit day, where the market has just about attained my price objective, I'll wait to bang out the position tomorrow morning on a strong opening.

In markets like these, you've got to be particularly calm and patient, and let the markets come to you. If you act subjectively or emotionally, your trading is bound to be irrational. The wilder and more volatile the market, the more important that you be absolutely calm and relaxed. And if you must sweat out a couple of bad days, well, that's the name of the game. Eventually, if your view of the market is correct and your timing is accurate, the market will move your way. And you'll score big, really big.

That's exactly what we've done with plywood. I put on a big line, at low prices—averaging under 90.00 basis March. It's been up, down, back and forth—and at this point, we have a $2,000-per-contract profit on a 50-lot position. Tomorrow morning I'll bail out and take another look at the market.

Friday, October 26

10:05 A.M.: Fridays are always my worst days. My positions are all going against me. And I nearly dislocated my shoulder trying to open the window. I can tell—this is going to be some day! Silver is down 250 points, cattle down almost 50. Looks like a better day for sailing than for trading. Well, Kroll, just sit tight for a while.

Plywood should open strong, and they can have my whole position—around 118.00 for March. The market is coming into overhead resistance, we have a $100,000 profit on the position, and the rally looks like it's about run out.

Noon: This morning's premonition was right. I see red lights clear across the board—new lows in most markets. Well, I've survived this kind of Friday before—hang on, kid, hang on.

C mailed me a bullish sugar article from one of the major London dailies. I got it before the opening and said, "Well, there goes sugar down today." It always spooks me to read bullish stories in the press, and sure enough, look at sugar, down 20 points on the day. Maybe they'll write a bearish sugar article next week, to get the price up again.

1:00 P.M. I ought to add some long silver right here. The market made new lows for the move and couldn't find any follow-through selling. The other internationals are starting to rally, and silver has dried up on the downside. It's ready to go. . . .

"How's March silver quoted?"
   "293.80 at 294.00."
   "Buy 20 Marches at the market . . . right, at the market."
   "Here I am. What's that? Bought 10 Marches at 294.00, and 10 more at 294.10. O.K., thanks."

Well, I just bought my 20 Marches; now I'll just sit back and relax. If the market closes strong, say over 298.00, I'll keep them. Otherwise I'll bang them out just before the close.

2:09 P.M. Silver has had a pretty decent rally, but the market's about to run out of steam. I don't feel like taking them home for the weekend—have a big enough position for now—so out they go.

2:10 P.M. O.K., I'm out of the silvers. Looks like the day trade netted about $2,000. Oh well, better luck on Monday.

Monday, October 29

It's a gray, rainy, cold, miserable day outside. That's just how the markets strike me, too. Good thing I closed out Friday's silver buys as day trades—the market's down 500 points now. If the volume dries up on this reaction, I'll start buying again. It's still a major uptrend, and the minor trend is just coming into some good buying support. Got to pick the spot carefully, though; don't want to be locked in on a sloppy buy decision.

Tuesday, October 30

11:30 A.M. (on the phone): "How's the market? I'm sorry you asked. It's terrible, absolutely *terrible!* You know, the last few days, everything was down, and there wasn't any news at all. Well, all the bearish news was saved up for this morning."
   All of it:
   Favorable crop news.
   Increased selling of newly harvested crops.
   Russia will harvest a record grain crop.

Argentina will start exporting soybeans.

Foreign demand is slowing for U.S. grains and soybeans.

And finally, reports from Peru indicate that anchovies are again breeding abundantly in coastal waters. (Anchovies are ground into a high-protein substance that competes in the world market with soybean meal. It's truly amazing—during the bull cycle in beans, there were no anchovies around. As soon as the bean market turns down, see how those clever little buggers know it's time to come back and start depressing the market again. What a game!)

3:30 P.M. Well, the battle smoke has cleared. Most of the markets hit new lows today and then staged a dynamite recovery. Cattle, for example, was down nearly the limit, then closed limit-up, for a 190-point trading range. Silver was down as much as 150 points but closed plus 350 on the day. I've been expecting this kind of violent turnaround—the news has been much too bearish and the markets have been generally oversold. We may not be starting major bull markets, especially in the Chicago items, but we've at least got a good recovery in front of us. On this rally, though, I'll close out some of our weaker long positions and reposition myself to take advantage of the next phase of the move.

Again and again it's demonstrated that you can't always anticipate the market action, no matter how tuned in you may be. But you must be cool enough that, if your positions run badly for a few days, you don't panic and lose them. If you really believe, on the basis of solid research and analysis, that the market will come back and offer you a better liquidating opportunity, just sit tight and bet on your own judgment. You'll usually be right.

Wednesday, October 31. (Halloween, trick or treat)

12:05 P.M. (on the phone to the Comex floor): "Listen, how are Dec and March silver quoted? Also, get me the silver volume, please."

"O.K., O.K., here I am. Dec is 288.60 bid, offered at '90. March is 293.40 bid. Volume is 2,700 lots so far."

"The market should be doing better than this, with all the

metals so strong. Silver should start moving up. Let me know if any volume starts coming in. Thanks."

1:00 P.M. (back to the floor again): "Look, please ask around to see what's the news on copper—it's really boiling. Also, what's doing with silver?

"Right. A Cities Service *force majeure* in copper. That's nothing—there must be more news than that. What about silver? I want to be right on top of it. What, you don't hear anything? Thanks, but keep me informed if anything comes up."

2:07 P.M. (to the floor): "Hello . . . sell 5 Marches at the market—no, wait, make it 10. That's right, I'm selling 10 March silver at the market. O.K., thanks."

2:20 P.M. (back to the floor): "Anything done to sell the 10 Marches? Sure I'm looking for my report. What's the matter, you guys fall asleep? Yes, 10 lots at the market. It closed 5 minutes ago . . . what's going on?"

"O.K., here I am. Sold 5 Marches at 293.00 . . ."

"Great, that's a good fill. What about the other 5?"

"Sold them at 292.70."

"Oh, well . . ."

"O.K., so I sold the 10 lots, right?"

"Right!"

Thursday, November 1

2:30 P.M. I should have stayed home today . . . can't make any sense out of this action. The markets opened unchanged, then had a vicious rally. Just as I was beginning to feel cosy and comfy, the stuff really hit the fan—new lows clear across the board. Well, O.K., I just leaned back in my chair and looked out the window for a while. And, what do you know! The sun came out again and . . . whammo! They're rallying again, closing unchanged on the day. Go figure it out!

"Look, will you get me the settlements on Dec, Feb, and April cattle? My board's not working, and I want to leave soon. Also, see if you can get any news on silver. Thanks."

2:50 P.M. You really have to be crazy to *want to* trade commodities all day. Why do I do it? Well, I made $27,000 last week —how's that for a good reason?

3:05 P.M. (on the phone with a nervous client): "What do I think of silver here? It's beautiful, that's what I think. Would I let my daughter buy it? Ha-ha, very funny!

"The market's really acting well . . . remarkably well. December was finding good support around 290.00. The market broke down on Monday and traded as low as 283.00, then stayed down there for a few more days. I think they were "suckering in" more shorts, that's what I think. Then today, it came steaming right back up and closed at 292.00, trapping all the sellers of the past few days. Silver's going higher . . . much higher . . . and pretty soon!"

3:15 P.M. Cushion just got back from Europe and said that the brokers there have been telling their clients to sell out their silver, and rebuy 20¢ lower. Ha! I wonder what they're saying now that the market's rallying? Shift to Eurodollars, I suppose. Last week's sellers are this week's buyers, covering shorts and scrambling to replace the long positions they were talked out of during recent weeks. At some point in the very near future, March silver will push right on through 3.18. And when that happens, it's 3.40 to 3.50 next stop. What'll I do at 3.40? Ha! I should have problems like that all the time.

Friday, November 2 (on the phone with Jarrett)

"Why is it Fridays are always my worst days? I ought to trade Monday through Thursday. Fridays, I should do something else, like play tennis or tune pianos. I just never make out on Fridays.

"What happened today? Well, they just sort of drifted down heavily . . . you know, *clunk!* Yes, my grain positions were down quite a bit. And cattle was doing fine in the morning but collapsed later in the session. Silver? That's the one bright spot. Right, we're holding 200 silvers, and they're acting fine.

"But here's the weekend coming up again, and we'll be out sailing in a few hours. They can't hurt me anymore till Monday."

Monday, November 5

The weekend newspapers had several full-page ads for all sorts of silver objects—bars, medallions, even plates—and it's starting to fuel a new bullish enthusiasm in the market. Whatever the real economics of the silver situation right now, this new psychological bullishness will tend to keep values firm. The market needed this new impetus to push up a potentially strong technical position. I bought 20 more silvers this morning on the lower opening. If the market closes strong, I'll keep them; otherwise I'll bang them out before the close and try again tomorrow. I already have my basic silver position, and won't add to it except on a strong close, where I can anticipate a bullish follow-through tomorrow. It's that extra edge that I want!

Soybeans were way down—they reacted 14¢ below last night's close, a real buying opportunity. I "counterattacked," and bought 50,000 bushels more. About a half hour later the market stabilized and then rushed up. It was incredible—it rallied 20¢ in little over an hour. But it closed about even on the day, so I kicked out this morning's purchase. It was a $6,000 day trade—not the worst day's pay.

Tuesday, November 6

Did I just make a stupid play! Really El Dumbo. I came in this morning, looking to buy May beans on a 3¢ or 4¢ lower opening, say around 5.30. My electric board showed May opening 5.29 to 5.30, so I hurriedly entered an order to buy 50,000 May beans at the market. It's a broad market, so I figured I'd get filled at 5.30, maybe 5.31. Well, the board had misprinted—May was actually opening at 5.34 to 5.38. And I paid 5.38 for my beans. As my daughter Bevie would say, "Rats!"

A close on the May beans over 5.50 would be very bullish and would make me stick with this morning's purchase. But if it closes lower, I'll kick them out just before the close. I already have a good-size bean position and I'm not inclined to add, unless the market closes strong. Otherwise, who needs another 50,000 bushels of aggravation tonight?

2:14 P.M. "Right, sold 50,000 May beans at 5.48. Thanks."

Wednesday, November 7

11:00 A.M. Ouch, this looks like a very expensive morning. The markets are opening much lower, and I'm heavily long. This type of action has all the earmarks of a classical bear trap—it's no wonder the specs usually lose. The market letters and advisory services have been bearish for weeks and have been strongly recommending short positions all over the board. This has built up a major short position of weak speculative traders, and I'm betting that we're within just a few days of an explosive upside rally that will really clean out all these new shorts.

Perhaps then another reaction, but the big play for the next few months, at least, will be on the long side. The bears have overplayed their hand and are about to be scalped. I'll take advantage of the next big rally—which could last a week or two—to scale out my long positions, and then try to accumulate some better long positions on the ensuing reaction.

3:10 P.M. Thumbtack just called and predicted that the energy crisis will put the stock market way down . . . at least to DJI 800. I'd better watch my markets extra carefully. During troubled times like these, when hardly anyone knows what to do, the sharp trader can really score.

Thursday, November 8

What's that? Beans up the limit? Sure, we're long a big position of Mays. Cattle up the limit, too. We're long Feb and April cattle, and I even bought 20 more Aprils on the lower opening this morning. I'll start scaling out the cattle right here, limit-bid. It's still a major downtrend, and I can't see it holding much above here.

Silver, which fell out of bed yesterday, is already plus 200 points and on the move. Even old fuddy-duddy corn is up 6¢. To-day's action bears out my thinking of the past few days—that the markets are due for a big recovery move. The commission house specs are predominantly short, and they're about to get nailed—again!

Friday, November 9

3:15 P.M. Know whose brain I'd like to pick? Armando the (Chief Peruvian) Anchovy, that's whose. It's absolutely amazing: beans were weak last week, and the news was the anchovies were "regrouping" and were ready for the catch. Well, O.K., beans were up the limit yesterday, and no news. After the close comes the report that lo! someone must have miscalculated. There were no anchovies for the catch, after all. Peru wasn't allowing any anchovy exports. Matter of fact, it almost seemed as though no one had ever heard of anchovies, that's how bullish the news re-lease was. So what do you think the market did today, following last evening's bullish report? Down the limit, of course! I'll bet tomorrow's reports will announce that the little buggers are back, leaping into the fishing nets in record numbers. What a game!

On the down-limit move, I bought more May beans. Looks like beans are coming right back into good support, around 5.40 to 5.45. I'm betting the market's going to hold—the people selling beans here are selling into a bag. They'll turn buyers at higher levels, like over 5.70.

4:00 P.M. (on the phone with Jarrett again): "What happened in silver today? It's funny, but I was just sitting here and thinking about that very thing. The annual year-end silver squeeze is com-mencing.

"The Swiss banks helped put the squeeze on Dec silver last year, and it worked for a week or so. Sure, they'll try the same trick again this year. Yes, it'll work again, I think. Dec was up 190 points, March up 110, May was plus 80 and July only up 30. Sept was unchanged . . . yes, I said unchanged. The switches are nar-rowing again, and I would expect to see Dec over Jan by the year end. I plan to take delivery on my Decembers, too—I think it's a good play because I can see an inversion sometime next year. No, of course I'm not sure . . . how can anyone be sure of that? But it's a good play."

Monday, November 12 (my last week before vacation)

10:35 A.M. The Chicago markets are tougher than they've ever been. There seem to be many more public speculators in these markets than ever before, and the weight of their buy and sell orders swings the markets wildly.

Friday afternoon the USDA came out with a bullish crop report on corn and beans. The market just opened with corn up 5¢, beans about unchanged, and cattle limit-up. I can't see the cattle holding at these levels, though. Too much selling pressure at this level.

12:10 P.M. The beans have had it for now. They're down 10¢ and don't show me any zip. Cattle is still limit-up, but it's reached my objective and is coming into heavy resistance . . . and the major trend is still sideways to down. I sold part of the cattle position, limit-up, yesterday, and I'll sell the balance right here. Am I relieved—it's only a small profit, not as much as I had anticipated; but when you've recovered from a big loss, with the trend against you, don't quibble about the size of the profit—get the hell out!

12:50 P.M. Corn's very strong, up 5¢ now. I'm not about to sell corn here—looks like it has plenty of momentum to move much higher, to over 3.00 for May.

12:55 P.M. We'll have to sit and sweat out the beans for a while. It sure acted poorly this morning, but beans will turn up, even though there's no telling when. It's not easy or comfortable to sit with the market moving against you, but sometimes you have to do it, temporarily. On the other hand, you can't be blindly stubborn; if the market action shows you that you're on the wrong side, you must respond by getting out. Whether you bail out immediately or wait for a better shot depends on your assessment of the near-term action, and how urgent you consider your predicament to be.

1:40 P.M. "Here come de beans," starting to move up. Patience pays off, it really does. May beans are now 5.44, unchanged for the day, although March is already up 3¢. I think we've seen the worst on beans; they had been down as much as 12¢ from last night's close, which means they've rallied 12¢ in the past 40 minutes—and that's power. Corn's starting to perk up again, too. The whole grain board is gathering steam now!

2:00 P.M. O.K., the grains are all roaring along. What a sight! Corn's up 10¢—locked up the limit. Beans have now rallied 18¢ from the lows, so they're up 6¢, and the day's not over yet.

Wheat has been in a solid base area for the past week. It wouldn't go down during the weakness of the past few sessions, so when the other grains started to rally and I saw wheat still doing nothing, I bought 100,000 bushels of May at the market—got the lot at 3.86. It's now about an hour later, and May wheat's trading around 3.93. I entered a 5¢ stop under my purchase, so I'm limiting my risk to about $6,000. But if the market closes above 4.00, then the trend will have turned up, and we'll really see fireworks. I like these odds: a $6,000 loss if I'm wrong, and a profit of perhaps $30,000 or more if I'm right. This should happen to me more often.

Tuesday, November 13

10:40 A.M. Well, what do you know! Looks like wheat is limit-up, right after we went and bought yesterday. That's like hitting a home run with the bases loaded—it's great when it happens, but don't hold your breath till the next time.

All the grains are strong today, and that's no surprise. They've been building up to this for the past few weeks. We're long a big line of wheat, corn, and beans; so go, go, go! Let's hear it for the grains!

11:10 A.M. (a conversation with Foxy, who's just returned from Geneva):

FOXY: Yes, I think M told me the truth. The Swiss banks have been heavy buyers of Comex silver, and December is the first big month of their position. He claims they're going to stand for delivery—really heavy delivery. That accounts for the large warehouse increases during November: the shorts know they'll be called for delivery, and they don't want to be caught, as he says, "with their pants down." Besides, some of the big shorts are hoping they can break the market now, so they can cover in the futures market and not have to make delivery. It's going to be a good battle!

SK: What do the numbers look like to him?

FOXY: I just called M again this morning. God, you have to get up in the middle of the night to get them during working hours. He said of course the warehouse stocks are increasing this month. About four months ago, the certificated stock of silver in New York increased from 51 to 56 million ounces, and then declined 46 million. The stock figure is back up to 53 million, and will increase to around 60 million. But he reckons that some 20 or 30 million ounces will be removed during the next few months—and that's over 2,000 contracts. He's still talking confidently about $3.50 to $4.00 silver during 1974.

SK: What about the story that some of the shorts have been borrowing silver for their certifications, and that they may be squeezed if the big longs take the bullion and put on the pressure?

FOXY: He doesn't know. Said that it's a damned good story, though, if true. He said that it's "common knowledge" that the reason the shorts are putting in silver bullion is because there's going to be a tremendous withdrawal. "Common knowledge," he says! "So," I said, "what does this make you think of the market?" Well, his "understanding"—and I like the way he used the words—his understanding is that "the interests that are buying are looking for a very major move on this thing."

SK: How much are they looking for?

FOXY: They are two- or three-year holders, looking for a minimum of $6.00 an ounce. I asked, "What's your feeling about 1974, in terms of supply and demand?" He said that the tremendous dealer-inventory depletion of silver bullion will be shown up on the next Bureau of Mines monthly summary.

SK: We should be getting that any day now.

FOXY: Right. He said there will be a tremendous inventory depletion. The deficit will be somewhere between 150 and 200 million ounces, depending on who you're talking to. He noted that people who say that the European banks have an excess of silver bullion in their vaults are talking nonsense. The banks expect to have more in their vaults next year, and even more the year after.

SK: But eventually, what will they do with all the silver?

FOXY: It's like the old sardine story. You know the sardine story, don't you?

SK: Sure—I see it in action all the time.

FOXY: It's about the man who had a warehouse full of canned sardines, which he sold for $50 a carton. The price went up to $70, and the new owner sold it, leading to a whole chain of buys and sells, profits and losses. Eventually the sardines "rallied" to $190 a carton, and the last buyer got stuck with them as prices plummeted. He decided to take his loss and just eat the sardines . . . until he discovered that they were rotten and were probably inedible all along. Hopping mad, he traced the entire series of transactions back to the original seller and confronted him with the fact that they were rotten. The first seller just eyed him coolly and said, "Listen, mister, those sardines were for trading—not for eating!"

SK: But listen, Foxy, won't the Swiss banks be sellers one of these days?

FOXY: Sure, they're sellers every day. They sell silver to Mr. A, and buy silver from Mr. B, but at generally higher and higher prices.

SK: But what makes you think that it'll keep going up? Even the sardines topped out and prices came down.

FOXY: You know, I can't imagine how you got so far in this business—you must have been lucky.

SK: Some luck! I never even won the prize in a Cracker Jack box. Listen, maybe those sardines weren't for eating, but neither is silver bullion.

FOXY: Right! Silver is for manufacturing, for hoarding, and for making money by buying futures and holding them. The total open interest in New York and Chicago futures—let's discount London for now, because the market's so thin— is approximately 1.6 billion ounces of silver. And there's only about 85 million ounces of certificated silver stocks backing such an enormous futures position. That's only about a 5 percent ratio, which is "rather low," as my friendly Swiss banker puts it.

Compare this silver inventory with gold, where there's some $50 billion available in world stocks, which someday could be thrown on the market. But the silver stocks . . . well, they've been diminishing every year, and they'll continue to diminish. M tells me the 85-million-ounce certificated stock position will be reduced at least by 50 percent during 1974.

We also discussed the Latin-American situation in silver. Peru, one of the world's major producers, is so short of foreign exchange because of the reduction in their fish-meal industry that they've already sold most of their silver reserves. And Mexico, too: we've seen a lot of Mexican silver being delivered on Comex during recent months—they've reduced their silver stocks to the bare minimum. Mexico is probably out of the picture as a seller of silver for at least a year.

SK: You know, it's amazing you're so gullible. Naturally the Swiss are bullish on silver. They're the big longs in the market, so it's obviously in their interest to see prices advance. You're lucky he didn't try to sell you Geneva Bridge.

FOXY: Look, I'm not gullible. If I find a source, a knowledgeable, inside source, I go with him. One must make a judgment

—the way you and I did last year, when we decided that copper was too cheap at 48¢. We looked at the high warehouse figures and said there'll be nothing left in a few months. Sure enough, 3 months later . . .

SK: I've got a nice little bridge right here you might be interested in buying. By the way, do you remember recently the big commission house that was projecting a 12¢ to 15¢ reaction in silver? Well, they hit it right on the nose, didn't they? There goes our theory that the big houses are always wrong. They were dead right on that one!

FOXY: Sure, but they'll keep trying to pinpoint the moves so minutely that they're sure to miss the major move when it happens. They're so concerned with churning out the commissions that they'll never hold onto a major position for the big move. They'll still be day-trading while the market is soaring.

SK: Well, that may be . . . but we won't, will we?

FOXY: That's for sure!

12:20 P.M. (on the phone with our Chicago broker): "Sold 45,000 bushels May corn at 2.58½, right. Sold another 65,000 at 2.58¾. Now, what about my final 15,000 at the market? Do you have that order? O.K. Look, it was entered at 12:02, and it's "only" 12:20 now. That's 18 minutes! I know you've asked. Please ask for it again."

Chicago is really slow in these wild markets. We used to get "filled" in four or five minutes—now it takes fifteen. You can die waiting.

1:10 P.M.: Silver's down again, on the news of a 3-million-ounce warehouse increase this morning. It's really a big fiddle. The silver market is going to move higher, much higher, and the specs are being fooled by all those warehouse increases. All the silver going into warehouse in November will probably be withdrawn early in 1974—and at higher prices, too. Then watch silver fly!

I wonder if there's anything to that rumor that some of the big silver shorts are borrowing silver to put into certificated warehouses, trying to depress prices so they can cover their shorts on the exchange. Daniel Drew, a famous nineteenth-century market operator, once said:

> He who sells what isn't hisn
> Must buy it back or go to prison.

4:30 P.M.: Well, the dust has finally settled, after a booming, busy day. Corn was up sharply, after being limit-up yesterday. I banged out one-quarter of my position, because the market had reached my intermediate objective and was starting to come into heavy overhead resistance. I'll sell some more, on strength, tomorrow.

Wheat looks poised for a big upward move, so I continued my no-loss stop on yesterday's purchase. I'll just keep following the market up for the time being.

On soybeans, I'm offering one-quarter of the position at 5.92 (for May). I wouldn't be selling any that low, except that I'm going away Friday and want to reduce positions somewhat. We averaged 5.60 on the purchase of the beans, and will sell the balance of the position on strength to the 6.06–6.16 level. The market may overrun that price—beans usually do overreact—but they'll subsequently drop back again, perhaps to the head-and-shoulders base area between 5.70 and 5.80. I'd like to rebuy the position there, buying 150 percent of the original long position.

On balance we're in good shape, really good shape. I've been scaling out my big grain long positions on strong advances, since I'll be away all next week. I'll be more confident being in a cash position. The markets will be around when I return, and I can always get back in then.

Wednesday, November 14

11:30 A.M. (another conversation with Foxy):

SK: What's the latest from your friendly Swiss banker?

FOXY: I spoke to M this morning. When I heard the news that gold had been set free and that central banks could now sell on the open market, I figured silver would be down at least 600 to 800 points at the opening.

SK: Who cares what you thought? What did he say?

FOXY: Well, M thought it was good propaganda and sound psychology, but he doesn't see any of the big banks selling gold. And the central banks—well, some of them have been selling on the open market all along. He doesn't think that this development will mean a thing to them, at least at current market levels. Why should the banks sell gold? To buy what? Yen? Francs? Dollars? Jelly beans maybe? Especially since they feel . . .

SK: What about buying dollars? The dollar looks strong.

FOXY: Sure, but the dollar is already up a lot. What are they going to do, chase the dollar? Why? Especially in the face of the so-called energy crisis. He did say that some of his people were thinking of getting out of gold, if it moves higher, and going into silver. And recall, he did predict the 40-to-1 gold/silver ratio last summer—and he was right there!

4:30 P.M. The markets are closed, and I'm sitting here trying to dope out some intelligent moves for tomorrow and the coming days—some good strategy for while I'm away next week. The grains are coming along fine—we've been long corn, beans, wheat, and cattle, and they've all been strong. I've been scaling out positions on strength. Now I'm completely out of cattle, partly out of corn; wheat was up the limit today, and I sold half my position. I haven't sold any beans yet, but the market will come up to my sell orders, and then I'll get my prices. I'm just afraid to follow these markets up on the long side, because basically I still see downtrends intact. If I don't sell the rallies into overhead resistance, where should I sell? On the declines?

Never be so worried about missing the beginning of a big move that you plunge into the market against your better judgment. The major trend, once it starts, lasts longer than most people expect. It's like a big, lumbering express train; once it gets up to top speed, it's awfully hard to reverse direction. Getting into a developing situation too early has always been one of my problems. Sure, it frequently works out O.K., but you really have to sweat it. It's not the best way to play the game.

Anyway, after I've sold out my long grain positions, if the major trend does subsequently appear to be turning upward, I'll be able to get back aboard on time. But if the rallies fail at these overhead resistance points, at least I'll be out of my positions and won't have to carry them down again.

It's just amazing how the news comes out well after the market has made its move. For the past four weeks, all the Chicago futures have stopped going down. But the brokerage firms continued bearish, all the market letters have continued bearish, and even the chart services were bearish. So, lo and behold, in the past two days the markets have surged upward, coming out of a good base area and trapping all the unwary speculative shorts. What's been causing the rally? No news at all . . . yet.

Well, we're just starting to see the news leak out, and what are the shorts supposed to do now? In today's *Wall Street Journal* there's a feature article that says, "Hopes for the leveling of food prices fade as fuel shortage results in lower output." The article goes on to talk about higher prices for grains, agricultural products, and livestock. Now, what do you do when you traded basically on the news and everything was bearish and you're short? And suddenly the market starts going up and you can't understand why. Well, brother, you're caught. Not only will you lose a bundle on your position, but you've missed out on a nice, cushy profit from a bull position.

This sort of thing just reinforces my feeling that it's fine to watch news developments and it's fine to study the fundamentals, but basically your trade timing should be predicated on technical factors. And when the technical situation clearly shows something at variance with the prevalent psychology of the market, you're better off getting out and standing aside, or else going along with the technical indicators. The news will come out later to support what's happened to prices—it always does.

Wednesday, November 28

10:00 A.M. (a phone conversation with my attorney): "Look— you know, that's really a very weak rationalization. You guys all have the naïve concept of stocks as "securities." What's so "secure" about a security? Franz Pick calls them "insecurities." All the stock investors I know are getting killed in the market, and my clients have tripled or quadrupled their money in the past two years. Now, my clients, if you ask them which is the riskier market, they might say that the stock market is riskier, at least from their personal experiences. It just depends on how you play it.

"Sure, you're right. Probably 80 percent of the public speculators lose money in commodity trading. But, they don't have to lose."

10:30 A.M. (phone calls to the floor and the Chicago broker): "Look, I'm waiting for buy reports on April cattle, from 47.67 down to 47.47. It opened lower—please chase after it."

"How did March silver open? Here I am. Opened limit-up. Pow! What's the news on the floor?"

"Anything on those cattle reports yet? I can fly out there and get my orders in the time it takes you to get them."

"Silver up the limit, huh? O.K., what's the news on gold, if that's what put silver up?"

Floor voice: ". . . now the European central banks and private banks are withholding sales, and they got a bunch of big speculators short—they'll have to run for cover. The gold market just shot right back up to where it was before the news came out about the central banks being able to sell on the open market. Sorry . . . gotta go!"

10.35 A.M. It's true—I really knew today would be a good day. You know how I knew? Well, I walk into the dentist's office this morning for my 8:30 appointment (only for him would I get up so early) and I'm feeling depressed, so I just sit down and open my mouth. Right away he starts poking around—you know, just before he goes in with the big needle. He looks a little draggy himself, right? Matter of fact, I don't really like the way *he* looks. Sure I'm concerned over his welfare, especially when he's standing over me with those "things."

So I say to him, "You know, you don't look so good this morning, Doc. What's up?"

"Oh, I feel terrible," he says. "I went to my dentist yesterday, and he pulled out two teeth."

"Serves you right," I say. Then he starts telling me all about *his* dental work yesterday (this I need at 8:35 in the morning?).

I say, "You know, you really look a little pale. Maybe you should sit down a minute. And you really shouldn't be starting work so early in the morning—can I get you a glass of water? And how about if we just cancel my appointment this morning?"

In the meantime, he's holding this big needle in his right hand. "Do you really mind?" he asks.

Do I really mind? "Doc," I say, "this is the best dental appointment I've had in years." So we rescheduled the appointment for two weeks later.

What was he fixing to do to me? I don't know, but whatever it was, good it wasn't going to be.

So as I walked out at 8:40, I felt wonderful. Boy, did I feel good. "Today's going to be a great day."

And it is . . .

10:42 A.M. (back to the Chicago broker): "Yes, here I am. Bought 10 April cattle at 47.60—what else? Bought 12 more at 47.60, O.K. Bought 2 more at the same price. Fine. Wait a minute . . . I want to get some more of the beauties—let's buy 10 more April cattle at . . . no, just buy them at the market. Right, at the market. O.K., thanks."

Victory at Sea, or, "Trading" from a Sailboat in the Virgin Islands

17

It's Monday, November 19, and I'm watching a mind-boggling sunset from the cockpit of our 41-foot chartered sailboat. We're snugly anchored in 20 feet of crystal-clear water, just off the beach of Great Harbor, on the island of Jost Van Dyke, British Virgin Islands. The joyous sounds of two of my daughters frolicking in the surf is music to my ears. And with ten-year-old Janet sitting in my lap, for the first time in months I'm relaxed . . . completely relaxed.

What the hell am I doing here, I wondered, nearly 2,000 miles from New York, completely isolated from the exchanges, phones, newspapers, and the myriad communications paraphernalia that habitually surrounds me? And who's minding the store, in this case the $2 million in cash, Treasuries, and commodity equities—one-third of it my own—that I manage on a fully discretionary basis?

Well, I'm here because I needed the break. No one can operate effectively and profitably in such a commodity arena, day in and day out, without an occasional battery charge. And, as to the little matter of who's minding the store—well, the market is.

(Could you please be a little more specific, Kroll?)

By way of background, let me say that people are frequently asking me if I think their market position is too large or too small.

116

Well, I've observed that when the market is going your way, the position is hardly ever big enough. You feel comfortable, knowing that the price trend is "working" for you—that the market is "watching over" your position. But when the market's going against you, the position is always too big, no matter how few contracts you may be holding.

So, since we had plane tickets to leave New York on Friday, November 16, and since these plans had been made some two months earlier, I had plenty of time to make arrangements for taking care of my store. Yes, the market would mind my positions. The plan was simplicity itself: I would keep open only those market positions where a vigorous and objective analysis indicated that I was on the right side of the market and that my risks were minimal. (Where practicable, I would enter no-loss stop protection, in case of a miscalculation.) Those of my positions which could not measure up to this examination were closed out.

Shortly before my scheduled departure, I surveyed my books and noted that I had the following long positions (there were no shorts at that time): May beans; May corn; May wheat; April cattle; December, March, and May silver.

Realistically and objectively, I assessed each position, arriving at certain strategic conclusions upon which my trading tactics were based. My examination of the five commodity positions was organized by breaking down each position into four areas:

1. Strategic Conclusions (written prior to my departure)
2. Trading Tactics (also written prior to my departure)
3. What Actually Happened (written upon my return)
4. Market Postscript (written one month after my return)

Let's see how it worked out.

May Soybeans

1. *Strategic Conclusions:* Major trend, down. Minor trend, sideways. The market is making a head-and-shoulders bottom, in the 5.20 to 5.60 area. It should uncover solid buying support between 5.20 and 5.35, and I would expect a strong upward move soon. A close above 5.65 would be very bullish, would trap all the shorts who sold in the 5.20 to 5.60 base area, and would indicate

that a new bull phase had begun. This surge through 5.65 should presage a sharp advance to the 6.10–6.20 level, from where I would expect a hefty reaction.

2. *Trading Tactics:* We are long a large position of Mays at an average price of 5.60. I would normally be reluctant to hold this position in the face of a major downtrend, but the decline has substantially attained my downside price projection and is in very solid buying support. Also, the head-and-shoulders bottom currently developing is a very potent bullish formation, and my view of the market is decidedly bullish. We will hold the long positions, with stop protection just under 5.30 (in the event of a disaster) and with the following sell orders entered "good till canceled":

> *Sell* one-quarter of the position at 5.92 (I wouldn't be selling this low if I weren't going to be away).
> *Sell* one-quarter of the position at 6.06.
> *Sell* the balance at 6.16.

Furthermore, on any subsequent decline to the 5.70–5.80 level, reinstate the long position, buying 150 percent of the original position. (Figure 24.)

3. *What Actually Happened:* The market closed firm on Friday, November 16, at 5.64, *just poised for the breakout.* Predictably, it gapped on Monday, opening at 5.70—which was to be the day's low—and closing at 5.78. *It had broken through*—now watch the shorts run!

The market did nothing but advance all week, closing on Friday at 6.31 bid (up the limit)—for a 67¢ rally from the previous Friday's close. Dynamite!

According to schedule, we sold one-quarter of the position at 5.92 on Tuesday, another quarter at 6.06 on the following day, and the balance on Friday's gap opening in the high 6.20s (the market had gapped through our 6.16 sell orders).

After seeing the results of this little exercise, I resolved to go away sailing more frequently.

4. *Market Postscript (written one month later, December 19):* I suppose you can always count on the bean market to exceed even the most liberal of price objectives, what with its amazingly large speculative following. The market rocketed through my 6.10–6.20 price objective, reaching 6.50 before the brakes were

Figure 24.

applied. A two-week trading range then developed, broadly between 6.15 and 6.50, but the selling pressure around the 6.20–6.40
level was clearly dominant. On Wednesday, December 12, May
beans closed at 6.28; two days later it had plummeted to 5.93—for
a two-day loss of 35¢. Here it is December 19, and the May beans
are still trading in the 5.90–5.96 area.

My trading tactics noted that after scaling out the long position, I would rebuy May beans (150 percent of the original position) in the 5.70–5.80 level. Well, that idea was predicated on a
sharp and sudden market break. Since the market didn't break
sharply but traded broadly in the 6.20–6.40 area—it could easily
be a major distribution area—I'm withdrawing my buy orders. The

Chicago grain market doesn't look like any great pillar of strength these days, so I'll just stay on the side for now. It might turn out to be a mistake, and maybe I'll miss a good move—but I'm not comfortable buying beans here, so I'll sit this one out. (Figure 25.)

May Corn

1. *Strategic Conclusions:* Major trend, sideways to up. Minor trend, up. I view the current extended trading range as a large continuation formation, out of which prices will ultimately move up. The market has retraced half the original bull move (rallied from 1.60 to 3.20, retraced down to 2.40), and should attract substantial buying support around the 2.40–2.50 level. The major trend will turn up on a close over 2.70, which I expect will happen soon. I look for the advance to peter out around the 2.90 level.

2. *Trading Tactics:* We are long 505,000 bushels May corn at an average price of 2.55. I think we're pretty safe on that position, considering the inherent and potential strength in the market. However, just to play safe, I'll enter a no-loss stop (sell at 2.56 stop), as the market is sufficiently liquid to take an order that large. If we're not stopped out, I'll leave a "good till canceled" sell order on the entire position at just above 2.80. If I do sell out the position at that price, which I expect to do, I'll rebuy May corn on a reaction back to the 2.60–2.65 support area. (Figure 26.)

3. *What Actually Happened:* The market closed on Friday, November 16, at 2.64. During the next three sessions, corn participated along with the other Chicago grains in a dynamic bull advance, culminating at the 2.86 level on the following Wednesday. It was a 22¢ rally in three days—not a bad move for corn. We banged out the entire position around 2.80 on that Wednesday.

My Trading Tactics notes that following the sale of corn, we'll rebuy May "on a reaction back to the 2.60–2.65 support area." Unlike the bean market, which kept trading near the highs of the move for two more weeks, corn virtually collapsed after hitting the 2.86 mark. Three trading days later, on Tuesday, November 27, May corn traded down to 2.57¾. This looked like pretty solid support to me, and I charged right back in on the long side, picking up some 200,000 bushels of Mays around 2.60.

A SOLD ONE-QUARTER THE
   POSITION AT 5.92
B SOLD ONE-QUARTER AT 6.06
C SOLD THE BALANCE IN THE
   HIGH 6.20's

Figure 25.

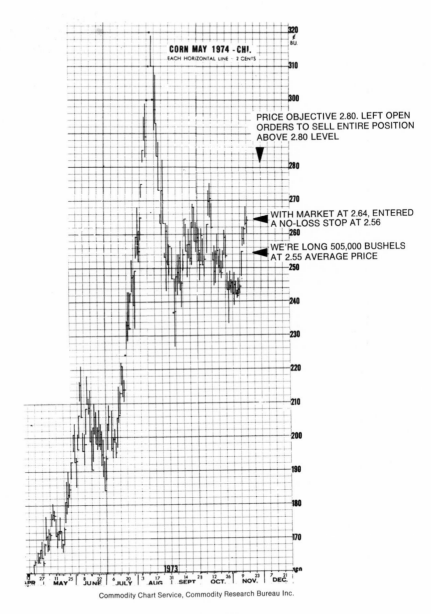

CORN MAY 1974 - CHI.
EACH HORIZONTAL LINE - 2 CENTS

PRICE OBJECTIVE 2.80. LEFT OPEN
ORDERS TO SELL ENTIRE POSITION
ABOVE 2.80 LEVEL

WITH MARKET AT 2.64, ENTERED
A NO-LOSS STOP AT 2.56

WE'RE LONG 505,000 BUSHELS
AT 2.55 AVERAGE PRICE

Commodity Chart Service, Commodity Research Bureau Inc.

Figure 26.

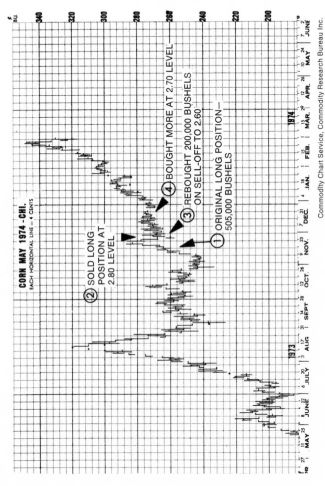

CORN MAY 1974 - CHI.
EACH HORIZONTAL LINE = 4 CENTS

② SOLD LONG POSITION AT 2.80 LEVEL

④ BOUGHT MORE AT 2.70 LEVEL

③ REBOUGHT 200,000 BUSHELS ON SELL-OFF TO 2.60

① ORIGINAL LONG POSITION— 505,000 BUSHELS

Commodity Chart Service, Commodity Research Bureau Inc.

Figure 27.

4. *Market Postscript* (*written one month later, December 19*): May corn has been locked within a broad trading range for the past three weeks, between 2.65 and 2.78. It keeps bouncing up from the 2.65 support level but can't seem to make it through the 2.77–2.78 resistance point. Following our 2.60 purchase, I added to the long position at the 2.70 level, bringing our average price to around 2.65.

I'm hanging in with the long position, because I view the major trend as up. The present broad trading range has all the earmarks of a continuation formation, out of which prices will ultimately move higher. A close over 2.80 would turn the trend decisively higher and would set up an upside price objective of 3.00 to 3.05. Depending on the intervening price action, I'll either scale out the entire position at that level or sell half the position, protecting the balance with stop orders below the market. (Figure 27.)

May Wheat

1. *Strategic Conclusions:* Major trend, sideways to down. Minor trend, sideways. Wheat looks less bullish than either corn or beans, but it could benefit from a general bullish psychology in all the grains. I'd expect May to find support around 3.80–3.90, but it should run into tough selling pressure on rallies to the 4.40 area.

2. *Trading Tactics:* We are long May around 3.86, bought right near the lows of the trading range. I just don't trust this market and don't believe that the major trend will turn up over the near term. I'll feel more comfortable closing out the entire position before I leave (although if I were staying, I'd probably sit with it). It's currently trading in the 4.10 area, and that looks good enough for me. Out it goes! (Figure 28.)

3. *What Actually Happened:* This is a simple one: I sold out half the position on November 14 at 405¾ and entered a protective stop order just below 4.00 for the balance of the position. On the following day, November 15, the market reacted, knocking off my sell stops at around 4.00. Oh well, we still made 16¢ net on the trade.

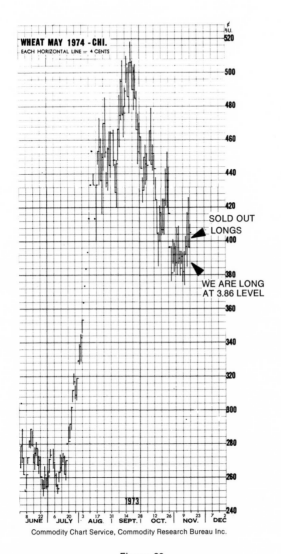

Figure 28.

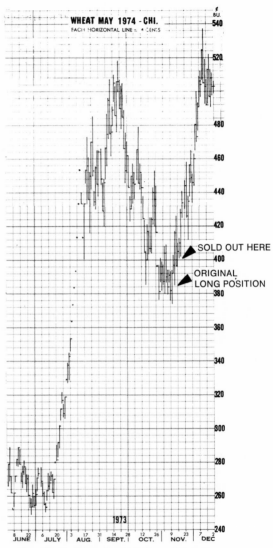

Figure 29.

4. *Market Postscript (written one month later, December 19)*: Talk about miserable timing—this one sets the record! Within just a few sessions of being stopped out at 4.00, May wheat commenced a fierce bull advance, carrying clear up to the 5.36 level on Wednesday, December 12, before faltering. Sure, I "caught" a 16¢ move ($800 per contract). But look what got away—the balance of a 136¢ move, equal to $6,800 per contract.

What went wrong? Well, rereading my Trading Tactics, I see that my major error was that I allowed myself to react emotionally and subjectively: for example, "I just don't trust this market," and, "I'll feel more comfortable closing out the entire position. . . ." My wheat position was bought near the lows and so was never really threatened. One of my principal trading philosophies, when initiating any position, has always been to assume that the market will experience a major move, and to "play" the position accordingly. (Naturally, the position should be protected in the event that it turns adversely—but as long as it's going your way, stick with it.) Had I adhered to that philosophy (you know what they say about hindsight—it has 20/20 vision), this position wouldn't have been liquidated so soon. (Figure 29.)

April Cattle

1. *Strategic Conclusions:* Major trend, down. Minor trend, sideways. This market looks like a bummer right now, although I can see it developing into a good bull deal later in the season. It is stuck in overhead around 50.00, the current price level, but should find support on declines to the 46.00–47.00 area. It will sure look strong on a close above 51.50, but I'm not holding my breath.

2. *Trading Tactics:* We're long April at a 46.00–47.00 average price. I just don't like the action, and the major trend is definitely down. For a while 50.00 looks like the top, whereas the market could easily drift back to the 47.00 level or even lower. I'll bang out the position here (49.00 to 50.00) and not have to worry about it next week. If the market drifts back to the 47.00 level, and I expect that it will, I'll get back aboard. (Figure 30.)

3. *What Actually Happened:* The market remained locked within the 49.00–50.00 range for two weeks, from November 12

Figure 30.

through 23, affording me the opportunity to scale out my long position at an average price of 49.40. We netted some 200 points profit per contract and, although I was anticipating a much bigger move, the market action "told me" to get out. Besides, I reasoned, I can always get back aboard if I find that I closed out prematurely. The extra round-trip commission is cheap insurance.

My Trading Tactics notes: "If the market drifts back to the 47.00 level, and I expect that it will, I'll get back aboard."

Well, the market did drift back there, and I did get back aboard.

Following the two-week 49.00–50.00 trading range, during which I sold out our rather substantial April long position, values tumbled right back down to the 45.00 support level, during the week of December 3. I reaccumulated a good-sized long April position, buying at 47.40 (on November 28), 46.60 (on November 30), and 45.57 (on December 3); I even managed to buy some at 45.00 (on December 4). Talk about scale-down buying!

So there we were, right back on the long side of April cattle. Let's shift to one month later, to see how the situation developed.

4. *Market Postscript (written one month later, December 19)*: We're back in the market again, at prices ranging from 47.40 down to 45.00. The market is still in a major downtrend. Prices had just fallen from 50.00 to 46.00, so a 50 percent return rally should fail around the 48.00 level. Interestingly enough, this 48.00 resistance level coincided with the chart downtrend line at around

Commodity Chart Service, Commodity Research Bureau Inc.

Figure 31.

48.40. So there we were—a major downtrend with a minor up-trend, and heavy overhead resistance between 48.00 and 48.40. What would you do?

My decision wasn't a difficult one: sell out the entire position above the 48.00 level.

We didn't have long to wait. On Monday, December 12, April cattle opened strong, at 48.00, and closed limit-bid at 48.47. The ideal way to sell out a position is into a strong market—this way you can enter scale-up sell orders, and the market comes to you. Well, we were certainly accommodated this time. Our April cattle position was closed out between 48.20 and 48.37.

I think we'll stay out of the cattle market for a while—looks like we can find more interesting possibilities in some of the New York markets. (Figure 31.)

Silver

1. *Strategic Conclusions:* Major trend, up. Minor trend, down. I especially favor this sort of market situation. It's dynamic! The market should continue to find good buying support around the 280.00 level, basis March, and will ultimately blast through the 292.00 (resistance) level. Very bullish action, and both the open interest and the volume figures support this bullish view. There is major selling resistance in the 310.00–315.00 area. In time, though, that will be penetrated, setting up a longer-term price objective of 340.00 to 360.00.

2. *Trading Tactics:* Silver's my baby (we're long some 210 contracts), and I'm not interested in trying to scalp the market at the risk of losing my position. The market is in equilibrium now, absorbing substantial selling pressure from both trade and speculative elements who are taking a near-term bearish view. I think they're wrong, and believe that it will be their buying, ultimately, that will put prices strongly higher. I see a very strong underlying tone to this market, which should soon become dominant. Look for much higher prices, so hold longs and enjoy! (Figure 32.)

3. *What Actually Happened:* I'll spare you the suspense—the finale of our amazing silver situation will be divulged in Chapter 18. The silver market was relatively quiet and subdued while I

Figure 32.

was away during the week of November 19, closing on that Friday at 287.50. This close was only 150 points higher than the previous Friday's close, and trading volume for the week was light. I returned to work on Monday, November 26, relieved to find the market so calm and that we hadn't made a single silver trade for the entire week. (When I'm right with a big market position, I invariably trade light or not at all.) My market view, as expressed in my Strategic Conclusions, remains unchanged—*extremely bullish!*

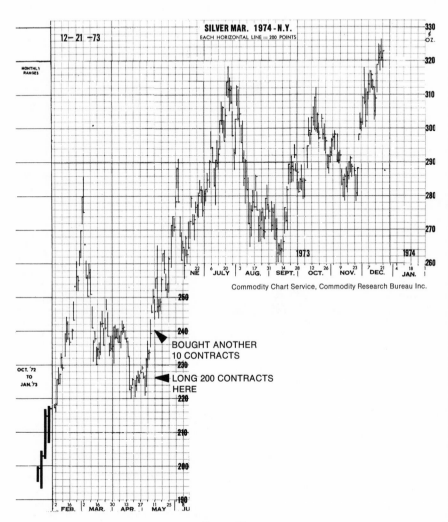

Figure 33.

4. *Market Postscript* (*written one month later, December 19*):
The market greeted my return on November 26 by falling apart
—closing at 280.80, down 670 points on the day. Some homecom-
ing! Of course the bears were in their glory, with the advisory
services "flashing" either bearish or, at best, neutral warnings.
Well, their glory lasted a whole 24 hours because, starting from
Tuesday's opening at 281.50, it took just six trading sessions for
the market to reach 318.00 (on Tuesday, December 4). A broad
two-week trading range then developed—a major test of en-
durance and cash between the bulls and bears—between 302.00
and 318.00 but the bears ultimately succumbed as prices attained
320.00 and then closed above that, for a new life-of-contract high
closing.

They Slide Faster Than They Glide, or, How We Dropped a Quick Million Dollars in Silver, and Then Made It Back, with Interest

18

When we last left our silver adventure in Chapter 10, it was May 29, 1973, with the market at 260.00,* and we had the following long position:

> 125 contracts @ 220.00 to 230.00
> 40 contracts @ 213.00
> 35 contracts @ 215.00 to 219.00
> 10 contracts @ 238.00

A total long position of 210 silver contracts—the relatively quiet start of a wild and wonderful adventure.

Riding a winning commodity position is a lot like riding a bucking bronco. Once you manage to get aboard, you know what you have to do—hang on and stay hung on; not get bumped or knocked off till the end of the ride. And you know that if you can just manage to stay in the saddle, you're a winner. Sound simple? Well, that's the essence of successful trading.†

That's simple enough, isn't it? We bought a lot of silver futures around Point (A) and projected that it would advance to 340.00–360.00. (In the interim I hoped to buy more silver, increasing the position to at least 300 contracts.) And we would

---

* Basis the July 1973 future.
† Page 44 of this book.

134

manage (sometimes just barely) to "hang on and stay hung on" till somewhere near the end of the ride.

Here's how it happened:

Points (A) to (B). The market extended its strong bull advance, attaining 291.00 (basis the March 1974 future)* on June 5. The rally fizzled against the previous life-of-contract high at 286.00 from three months earlier. Silver seems to have a tendency to fail against previous contract highs—sometimes just penetrating the previous high, attracting considerable speculative covering and new buying, and then failing.

Points (B) to (C). On the failure against the 286.00 level, I was very keen to add to the long position. But at what level? The market was becoming increasingly volatile, and I didn't want to jeopardize my existing position—held at excellent prices—by carelessly or imprudently pyramiding on the bull advance. (Figure 35.)

Well, the market had just advanced some 70¢, from 220.00 to 290.00. A 50 percent retracement (35¢ decline) would carry down to 255.00, which would also coincide with pretty solid support in the 250.00–260.00 area. There was my buy zone. I entered scaledown buying orders from 265.00 to 255.00, and during the week of June 11 I accumulated another 70 contracts. This brought our total long position to 280 contracts.

I felt very good about it. We were long in a powerful, confirmed bull market, and had just increased our position on a minor-trend reaction back into support. I now projected that the market would resume its advance from the current 255.00–265.00 support level, eventually attaining and sundering the 286.00–290.00 resistance top. This would establish our intermediate-term price objective at 315.00 to 320.00, and our longer-term objective at 340.00 to 360.00. This was pretty heady stuff! (Figure 36.)

Points (C) to (D). On June 11, the market traded as low as 255.50; but on July 24—just six weeks later—it had reached 318.20. During this advance, the market did fail (temporarily) against the 286.00–290.00 resistance level, reacting all the way down to 277.30 on July 11. But it was a bull deal, and the upward mo-

---

* All price references from here on will be basis the March 1974 future unless otherwise specified. (See Figure 34.)

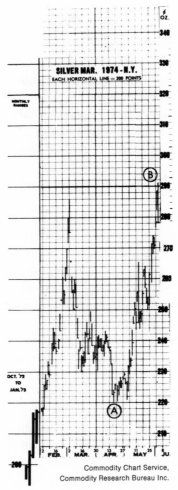

Figure 34.

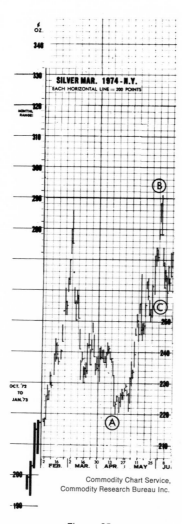

Figure 35.

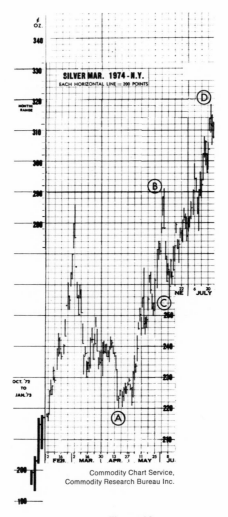

Figure 36.

mentum was sufficient to keep the market on its original course, minor technical reactions notwithstanding.

I was in something of a quandary when I saw prices zooming into our 315.00–320.00 intermediate-term price objective. What to do? Granted, the market was in a powerful bull trend, and who could predict where the ultimate top would be? (Memories of my past soybean and wheat fiascos were fresh in my mind; I could almost hear little voices saying, "Hold on! Sit tight!") On the other hand, there was an emotion compounded of greed and fear that constantly reminded me, "Bulls make money, bears make money, but hogs always lose." Was I being too much of a hog? Perhaps.

So I decided to play it safe (in a manner of speaking—because who could ever claim to be playing it safe sitting with 280 silver contracts in this kind of market?), and entered sell orders for one-third the position at 319.00 to 322.00. This, of course, is very much in accordance with my general trading principles.

Of course I never got any of these sell orders off, because . . .

Points (D) to (E) from the 318.20 rally high the market plummeted to 287.90 in just four sessions, and then . . .

Points (E) to (F) rallied right back to 312.70 on August 1, failing against the previous 314.00–318.00 top area. (Figures 37 and 38.)

Points (F) to (G). Have you been wondering where we lost the million (of paper profit)? Well, it was right here. How'd you like to lose all that money "between" (F) and (G)? That's where we lost it. There's an old saying in this business, "No one ever makes money in commodity trading; they just lend it to you till you give it back." Well, here's where my little group gave back our million dollars of paper profits. (Figure 39.)

In the six-week period from August 1 to September 11, the market traded from 312.70 down, down, down, down . . . all the way to 260.50.

I can't say who was more shocked and amazed, my clearing broker or myself (or maybe even my managed accounts—although I "managed" to avoid listening to their advice during the worst part of the slide). This market reaction represented nearly instant evaporation of some one million dollars of my clients' and of my own hard-earned funds.

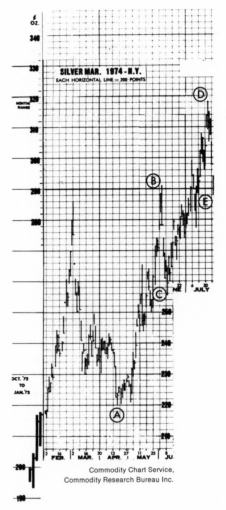

Figure 37.

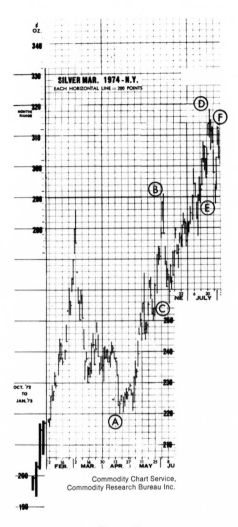

Figure 38.

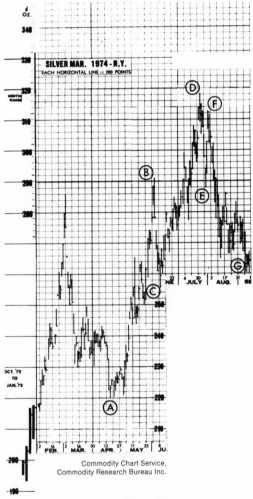

Figure 39.

The market should have held around 286.00–290.00, which had been the former-overhead-resistance-now-turned-support-area. Well, prices rocketed down through this support level like a shot, simply devastating the beleaguered longs—and lending considerable paper profits to the shorts. If 286.00–290.00 couldn't hold, where was the next logical support level? I wasn't very happy about this one, but I had to face reality: the next support wouldn't be before 265.00–275.00. *Ouch!*

This projection proved right, but only briefly. On August 14, March silver traded down to 265.00 and then rallied all the way back to 283.40 on August 30. That's what I would call more bounce to the (troy) ounce. But my relief was to be short-lived. After trading between 265.00 and 280.00 for some four weeks (had we weathered the storm?), the market collapsed on Monday, September 10, and hit 260.50 the following day.

I'd like to describe to you how I stood there, on that final break, buying my head off. Well, I'd sure *like* to tell that story—but I can't, because that's not what happened. Much to my subsequent chagrin, during that wild week I sold off some 90 of my 280 silver contracts. I even had to reach over my Jesse Livermore book—which once again had been placed in front of my floor phone to discourage irrational and subjective trading—but even that didn't prevent me from selling. I kept telling myself how bullish I was, and I kept rereading my bullish notes and price projections; so why did I sell those 90 contracts?

First of all, I was scared (I'm not experienced at losing more than a million dollars so abruptly). I was discouraged that the market hadn't acted as per my projections. I felt the need to get into a more liquid position to meet the seemingly continuous flow of margin calls (we were being called twice daily while the market was breaking). And I was absolutely determined to defend as much of the long position as I could afford to defend. Well, what more can I say? Just this—I hope I never have to live through that sort of thing again.

Points (G) to (H). Some 23,354 silver contracts (representing 38 percent of the total open position) were traded that week, between 260.50 and 266.00, with massive long liquidation plus very heavy new short selling that completely battered the market. (Figure 40.)

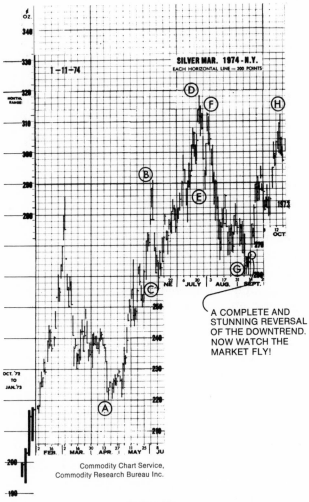

A COMPLETE AND
STUNNING REVERSAL
OF THE DOWNTREND.
NOW WATCH THE
MARKET FLY!

Commodity Chart Service,
Commodity Research Bureau Inc.

Figure 40.

But a very intriguing realization dawned on me Friday afternoon, September 14, about two o'clock. The market was acting as if it was about to close on the highs of the day—but more than that, at the highs of the entire week. What's so significant about that? Just this: every contract sold during that entire week of panic had been sold *lower* than the final closing for the week.

I had just a few minutes to assess the situation, and it came down to this: a complete and stunning *reversal* of the downtrend. The market was on the verge of a major rally, and besides the new buyers who would be bidding the market back up, there were some 23,000 contracts of silver sold during that week that would probably have to be bought back—at sharply higher prices.

I knew what I had to do. I had to get back in and start buying. I managed to pick up 50 contracts in the last few minutes of trading, at several cents higher than where I had so recently sold my contracts—but it could have been worse. At least I got back more than half of what I had sold, which brought my long position back to 240 contracts.

From that Friday's close, at 266.50, the market embarked on a fantastic display of bullish enthusiasm, hitting 312.00 on October 17, just five weeks later. Well, here we were at the contract highs again . . . but would it go through this time?

Points (*H*) *to* (*I*). Not yet—it still wasn't ready. The selling pressure at the contract highs once again predominated, sending the bulls reeling and dispatching prices earthward once again. (Figure 41.)

But this time I would be in position to buy on the reaction. But where? Well, the market had just advanced some 52¢ (who can keep up with these crazy, wild swings?), from 260.50 to 312.00. A 50 percent reaction from the 312.00 top would bring values down to the 286.00 level.

And I was there—holding out a bushel basket, bidding for 70 contracts between 284.00 and 288.00. And I bought the whole lot, which brought our position up to 310 contracts—the largest silver position we'd ever held.

The market looked really bullish now, having absorbed and repelled the enormous selling pressure that both the shorts and the "weak" longs had brought to bear. The market was technically

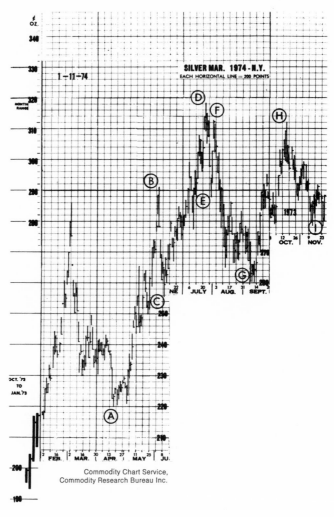

Figure 41.

strong, and it even had some really top-notch bullish stories going for it, too. Examples:

1. The Swiss banks were going to squeeze the nearbys. (It was an old story, but it always seemed to work, especially while the market was moving up.)

2. A Texas multimillionaire was planning to take delivery on a minimum of 20 million ounces of silver (2,000 contracts) against the about-to-expire December future.

3. A major Italian chemical company was going to pull 10 million ounces of bullion out of certified warehouse stocks.

4. One of the major Chicago grain dealers was heavily short silver and was being squeezed by other professional operators.

I was more impressed with the action of the market than with the stories (although I certainly did enjoy watching them push the market higher and higher), and the action "told" me that the long side of the market had shifted from weak to strong hands. The next test of the contract highs should prove successful, and I was anticipating a speedy resumption of the great bull advance.

Points (I) to (J). And that's exactly what happened. March closed at 288.20 on November 27, opened on a mighty gap at 298.20 on the following day, and closed limit-bid—up 1,000 points —at 298.20. Within four more days, it had hit 318.00. (Figure 42.)

Points (J) to (K). From 318.00, the market suffered a stunning reversal, declining to 300.20 on Wednesday, December 5. This abrupt and unexpected reaction was to be the final assault attempt by the bears, as well as the last opportunity for many of the commission-house speculators to sell out their long positions, *on weakness* (of course), right before the market orbited into space. Up, up, up and away . . . with the bulls firmly in command. At the close on Tuesday, January 8, March silver stood at 343.70 It had made it! (Figure 43.)

I can't possibly describe how relieved I felt to see the market advancing into my projected selling zone. After having held silver for more than a year for both my managed accounts and myself, and having suffered (that should be spelled with a capital "S") mightily, through the ups and downs of this wild, volatile market, it felt really good to see prices moving up to and through my resting sell orders.

Now, having sold out some 160 contracts (about half the total

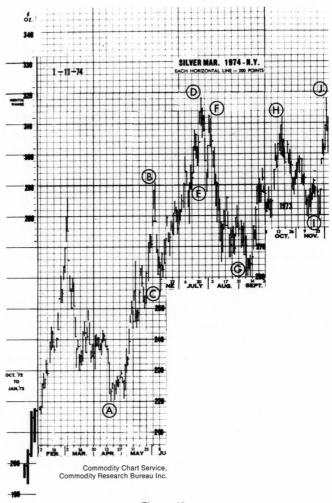

Figure 42.

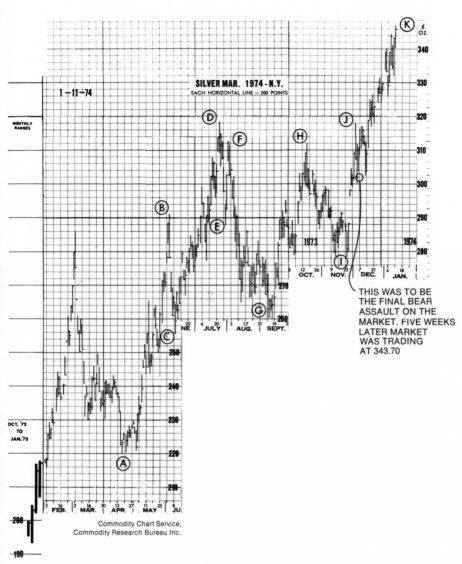

Figure 43.

long position), between 340.00 and 344.00, I was faced with the decision regarding the balance of the position. Sitting with the remaining 150 contracts, in effect *doing nothing*, really involved *doing something*. It involved the conscious decision to be long 150 silvers at the 340.00-plus price level. Or, as I asked myself, would I go out and buy 150 silvers here?

The answer was a resounding no. The market had attained my upside price projection—which, by the way, had been corroborated by several unrelated price "counts." The last time I neglected to sell, under similar circumstances, I had to sit through a 50¢-plus decline, and memories of that debacle were still fresh in my mind. Besides, I was just worn out from the whole tense year of silver sitting and anxious to be on the sidelines for a while.

My mind recalled a number of trading maxims (some of them my own), both encouraging me to hold the balance of the position and telling me to sell out. I realized that I should stay aboard, and that I'd probably regret what I was about to do. But I decided to "sell down to a sleeping level," which, in this case, was to a zero position. With a sigh of relief, and a vow not to weaken the next time, I sold out the balance of our position. It had been quite a ride!

After the smoke had cleared, my back-office manager, Ralph, calculated that we had recovered the million dollars of profits surrendered during the late great market collapse, plus a bonus of some $300,000. In total, then, we had taken some $1.3 million out of silver in less than two years.

Had it been worth the aggravation? Well, I understand that my clients indulged in considerable new luxuries with their profits. And my new boat is called *Quicksilver* (affectionately nicknamed the QS-1), courtesy of the you-know-what market. Yes, it was well worth it!

Epilogue

A prominent Swiss banker once described the futures market as the great equalizer of wealth. He noted how quickly and substantially it rewards the "clever operator" and just as abruptly penalizes the careless or inept trader, in the most direct way known to our capitalistic society—through his checkbook.

It's often said that in any financial endeavor, it takes money to make money. That may be true in general, but in commodity trading it doesn't necessarily take much. Careful and thorough research combined with accurate trade timing is far more important than a big starting bankroll. Consider the case of account No. 11 in "Summary of Managed Accounts" at the end of the Preface, whose capital appreciated from $2,565 to $113,191 in less than two years. And just to ensure that he didn't "give back" his profits, No. 11 withdrew $22,500 from the account—almost ten times his original investment—still leaving him with a trading equity of $90,000.

And he's not the only one to score such a financial coup: take accounts No. 1 (from $17,460 to $127,889), No. 2 (from $10,000 to $72,176), No. 8 (from $16,735 to $93,080), and especially No. 17, whose trading account appreciated from $15,000 to over $140,-000 in just sixteen months.

On the other hand, the annals of futures trading are littered with the unfortunate tales of people who lost substantial fortunes, in many cases more than they actually had. The point is clear: if your timing is bad, or if you trade carelessly or unintelligently, you're sure to lose a great deal of money—perhaps all your money (or even more!).

And while it's much easier, and statistically more likely, to join the losing side, let's review what it takes to get into—and stay in—the very exclusive winners' circle.

1. First of all, make a realistic appraisal of your objective in trading commodities. Is it to engage in an exciting and dangerous speculative game, or to make lots of money? If the former, I strongly urge that you take up sky diving or do a round-the-world trip; either will be much more exciting and considerably less expensive. If the latter, be assured that you'll have to work long, hard, and seriously at it.

2. Now let's get down to business. If you're going to be a winner, you'll have to study the various factors which influence each market, learn the mechanics of trading, and make an in-depth study of technical analysis. Most important of all, you'll have to develop *and practice* patience, objectivity, determination, and courage. I don't have to elaborate on this point, since I've been talking about it for the past eighteen chapters.

3. Isolate and identify the major and minor price trends of each market and play just for the major moves. Selectivity is the name of the game, and you should restrict your trades to those situations which lie in the direction of the major market trend— that's where the big money lies. Let your buddies experience all the fun and excitement of scalping and day-trading the markets; in the meantime you can be thinking of what you'll name your yacht or where your new summer home will be. Just be patient and confident that your investment approach is right. You don't have to take my word for it—the market will prove it to you, in a very satisfying and profitable way.

4. When you do initiate a position, premise that you're aboard for a major move and play it accordingly. Don't engage in any trades or close-outs because of boredom or impatience. Get aboard and stay aboard for the ride, which invariably lasts longer and goes further than you'll ever anticipate. Certainly if you're wrong —and the market (or the margin clerk) will tell you that, too—get

out and do it quickly. But let Dickson Watts's adage, "Run quickly, or not at all," be the one and only reason for getting out early in the game.

There is a well-known axiom in chess: white plays to win, black plays to draw. Simply stated, this means that since white plays first, it is deemed to have the advantage (we are assuming a contest between two equal players) and plays an aggressive game aimed at winning. Black, on the other hand, is at a disadvantage and therefore begins by playing defensively, being satisfied with a draw—that is, unless white blunders and allows him to secure the offensive.

Apply this maxim to futures trading: when ahead, with the market moving favorably, play for the big score and don't settle for a minor profit. On the other hand, when you are sitting with a losing position and know that the position is contrary to the major market trend, seek a "draw." That is, spend your constructive effort in calculating how to close out the losing position with a minimum loss or perhaps a modest profit—and if such an opportunity is offered, take it. This is more realistic than and far preferable to playing the wishful-thinking game and still trying to make big money on every losing position. It's more likely that you'll make your big money on a position where you're in step with the major trend.

5. Next to being able to isolate and identify the prevailing market trend, the critical necessity is to time your trades accurately. I've often read, in the trading handbooks distributed by the large commission houses, how a speculator can be right on just a small fraction of his trades and still be a big winner. I can't argue with their logic, but I find their conclusion very hypothetical. The winningest accounts I've seen still manage to chalk up some mighty big losses—it seems just about impossible to always keep losses small, no matter how hard you try—but they are able to score on better than 50 percent of their trades. In some cases, the batting average is closer to 70 percent. So if you make money on less than half of your trades, you should work to improve your percentage. Trade less and be more patient and discriminating in zeroing in on positions.

6. My final piece of advice—and I am very mindful of it in my own operation—is to KEEP THINGS SIMPLE. That applies

to every aspect of your dealing: your market and research approach, your timing and price objective studies, and even your tax-straddle trading.

An experience of mine springs to mind. It was late December of 1972, and I was accumulating a large copper position around the 48.00¢ to 50.00¢ level. (This was described in Chapter 5.) One morning a very elegant and professional-looking man called at my office and gave me his card. He represented a well-known private banking group, with an excellent reputation in the financial community. After the requisite small talk, he got to the point of his visit:

X: We understand you are a large buyer of copper on the Commodity Exchange.

SK: Well, that may be. What can I do for you?

X: May I ask you why you're buying copper at this time?

SK: I would think my actions speak for themselves. I'm looking for copper prices to advance substantially.

X: Uhm . . . (pause) . . . Uhm . . . well, we have an extensive study of the world copper situation, and we'd appreciate having your opinion of it.

(He handed me the study, bound in a neat portfolio. I thumbed through it while he scrutinized me closely. It had been prepared by some prominent economists, and looked very complicated and altogether too theoretical.)

SK: Frankly, I don't really understand much of this. I think it's much too complicated—has too many variables—to be of much practical help in trading copper profitably. If you want my opinion, I'd prefer a more basic, objective approach to the market. But what do your people make of it?

X: We are extremely impressed with the depth of the study, and with their statistical models. We have decided to avoid the market now, and will wait till late 1973 before starting to buy.

I don't want to prolong the story unduly. Suffice it to say that my banker friend left me a copy of the copper study (it's still on the shelf behind my desk) and departed. A more detailed reading of its contents that evening confirmed my original conclusion.

Well, the rest is history. Yes, there *was* too much copper in London warehouses—much too much. And this enormous inventory *was* weighing on the market. And no one could have imagined—least of all my banker friend or his fancy economic study—how this enormous surplus could be consumed over the near term. I couldn't either, for that matter, but that didn't trouble me. The market action "told" me in no uncertain terms that prices were heading higher, and my strategy was based on that. Let the others worry about *why* it may go up—they'll still be pondering long after the move is under way.

What actually happened is very simple. One day a Chinese trade group arrived in London, and when they went home, they took all the copper back with them. Suddenly, no more copper!

And a year later, when my banker friend was planning to buy his copper, it was selling at $1 a pound.

I've already told you the moral of this story: *keep things simple.*

And if anyone who reads this book wants to take the time to come up and see how complicated a research study can be, I'll be glad to show you the one that Mr. X presented to me—it's a real doozy.

GOOD LUCK!

Appendix

This appendix contains additional technical information which will supplement the body of the book and can be used as a reference. Basically, it covers the various commodity futures traded on each exchange and discusses such diverse aspects of the business as opening an account, commodity regulation, price analysis, trading techniques, and commodity put and call options.

Briefly, in this book we are dealing with commodities and commodity futures. A *commodity* is an article of trade or commerce, a tangible product as distinguished from a service. It may be something that we wear (wool, cotton, or dacron), that we walk upon (cement or plywood), or that we eat (apples, bacon, beef).

A *commodity future* is a contract (to buy or sell a specified commodity) which is traded for future delivery, on an organized and licensed commodity futures exchange. These exchanges, listed below, establish rules and regulations for the conduct of trading, including trading hours, size of each contract (called a unit of trading), and minimum commission charges and margin rates.

A *futures contract* is a legal instrument that binds both the buyer (the "long") and the seller (the "short") to the following obligations: The buyer must either sell (offset) his long position or accept delivery of the cash (actual) commodity during the delivery month for the contract. The seller, unless he has previously closed out (bought) his short position, must deliver the cash commodity during the delivery month for the contract.

FUTURES TRADING FACTS

Following is a compilation of the commodity exchanges of North America, together with pertinent contract and commission data for the commodities traded. The table is up-to-date as of early 1974 but is subject to change. (In the past, at infrequent intervals, some of the exchanges have announced minor changes in trading hours, commission rates, etc.)

COMMODITY	NAME OF EXCHANGE Trading Hours—N.Y. Time Mon. thru Fri.	CONTRACT	MINIMUM FLUCTUATION Per Lb., etc.	Per Contract	ROUND TURN COMMISSION Domestic Non-Member
BROILERS, ICED**	Chicago Board of Trade 10:15 A.M. - 2:05 P.M.	28,000 Lbs.	2½/100¢	$7.00	$30.00
CATTLE, LIVE BEEF (Midwestern)	Chicago Mercantile Exchange 10:05 A.M. - 1:40 P.M.	40,000 Lbs.	2½/100¢	$10.00	$40.00
COCOA*	New York Cocoa Exchange 10:00 A.M. - 3:00 P.M.	30,000 Lbs.	1/100¢	$3.00	$60.00
COCONUT OIL*	Pacific Commodities Exch. 10:30 A.M. - 2:15 P.M.	60,000 Lbs.	1/100¢	$6.00	$33.00
COFFEE "C"*	N.Y. Coffee & Sugar Exch. 10:30 A.M. - 2:45 P.M.	37,500 Lbs.	1/100¢	$3.75	40¢ — 49.99¢ $60.00 / 50¢ — 74.99¢ $70.00
COPPER*	Commodity Exch., Inc. N.Y. 9:45 A.M. - 2:10 P.M.	25,000 Lbs.	5/100¢	$12.50	$36.00 + 50¢ Exchange Fee
COTTON* #2	New York Cotton Exchange 10:30 A.M. - 3:00 P.M.	100 Bales (50,000 Lbs.)	1/100¢	$5.00	$45.00 when price is under 40¢ Add $5.00 for every 5¢ rise thereafter
EGGS, SHELL (FRESH)*	Chicago Mercantile Exchange 10:15 A.M. - 1:45 P.M.	22,500 Doz.	5/100¢	$11.25	$40.00
Grains—Chicago* WHEAT, CORN, OATS, SOYBEANS	Chicago Board of Trade 10:30 A.M. - 2:15 P.M.	5,000 Bus.	Oats 1/8¢ / Others 1/4¢	$6.25 / $12.50	$25.00 / $30.00

* Special rates for Straddles and Day Trades.

** Special rates for Straddles.

* Special rates for Straddles.

Source: Commodity Research Publication Corp., New York City.

COMMODITY	NAME OF EXCHANGE Trading Hours—N.Y. Time Mon. thru Fri.	CONTRACT	MINIMUM FLUCTUATION Per Lb., etc.	Per Contract	ROUND TURN COMMISSION Domestic Non-Member
WHEAT —Minneapolis	Minneapolis Grain Exchange 10:30 A.M. - 2:15 P.M.	5,000 Bus.	1/8¢	$6.25	$30.00
WHEAT —Kansas City	Kansas City Board of Trade 10:30 A.M. - 2:15 P.M.	5,000 Bus.	1/4¢	$12.50	$22.00
Grains—Winnipeg OATS, RYE, RAPESEED, BARLEY, FLAXSEED	Winnipeg Commodity Exch. 10:30 A.M. - 2:15 P.M.	5,000 Bus. / 1,000 Bus.	1/8¢	$6.25 / $1.25	5,000 Bus. $25.00-Rapeseed, Flaxseed / 5,000 Bus. $20.00 - Oats, Barley, Rye / 1,000 Bus. $ 4.50 [Canadian Prices] / Flax : 1,000 Bus. $5.50
HOGS, LIVE*	Chicago Mercantile Exchange 10:20 A.M. - 1:50 P.M.	30,000 Lbs.	2½/100¢	$7.50	$35.00
LUMBER	Chicago Mercantile Exchange 10:00 A.M. - 2:05 P.M.	100,000 Bd. Ft.	10¢/1000 Board Ft.	$10.00	$40.00
MERCURY*	Commodity Exch., Inc., N.Y. 9:50 A.M. - 2:30 P.M.	10 Flasks (76 Lbs.)	$1.00	$10.00	$40.00 + 50¢ Exchange Fee
MILO*	Chicago Mercantile Exchange 10:30 A.M. - 2:15 P.M.	400,000 Lbs.	2½/100¢	$10.00	$40.00
ORANGE JUICE** (Frozen Concentrated)	New York Cotton Exchange 10:15 A.M. - 2:45 P.M.	15,000 Lbs.	5/100¢	$7.50	$45.00
PLATINUM	N.Y. Mercantile Exchange 9:45 A.M. - 1:40 P.M.	50 Ozs.	10¢	$5.00	$45.00 + $2.00 Clearance Fee
PLYWOOD	Chicago Board of Trade 11:00 A.M. - 2:00 P.M.	69,120 Sq. Ft.	10¢/1000 Sq. Ft.	$6.91	$30.00

* Special rates for Straddles and Day Trades.   ** Special rates for Straddles.

(CONTINUED)

FUTURES TRADING FACTS (continued)

COMMODITY	NAME OF EXCHANGE Trading Hours—N.Y. Time Mon. thru Fri.	CONTRACT	MINIMUM FLUCTUATION Per Lb., etc.	Per Contract	ROUND TURN COMMISSION Domestic Non-Member
PORK BELLIES	Chicago Mercantile Exchange 10:30 A.M. - 2:00 P.M.	36,000 Lbs.	2½/100¢	$9.00	$45.00
POTATOES*	Maine-N.Y. Merc. Exch. 10:00 A.M. - 1:30 P.M. Idaho Russet-Chicago Mercantile Exchange 10:00 A.M. - 1:50 P.M.	50,000 Lbs. 50,000 Lbs.	1¢ 1¢	$5.00 $5.00	$30.00 $30.00
PROPANE GAS (LPG)	N.Y. Cotton Exchange 10:05 A.M. - 3:10 P.M.	100,000 Gals.	1/100¢	$10.00	$40.00
SILVER	Commodity Exch., Inc., N.Y.* 10:00 A.M. - 2:15 P.M. Chicago Board of Trade** 10:00 A.M. - 2:25 P.M.	10,000 Troy Oz. 5,000 Troy Oz,	10/100¢ 10/100¢	$10.00 $5.00	$45.00 + 50¢ Exchange Fee $30.00
SILVER COINS	N.Y. Mercantile Exchange 9:35 A.M. - 2:15 P.M.	$10,000 face amt. (dimes, quarters and half dollars)	$1.00 bag	$10.00	$35.00
SOYBEAN MEAL**	Chicago Board of Trade 10:30 A.M. - 2:15 P.M.	100 Tons	10¢	$10.00	$33.00
SOYBEAN OIL**	Chicago Board of Trade 10:30 A.M. - 2:15 P.M.	60,000 Lbs.	1/100¢	$6.00	$33.00
SUGAR #10 (RAW)* (domestic)	N.Y. Coffee & Sugar Exch. 10:00 A.M. - 2:50 P.M.	50 Tons (112,000 Lbs.)	1/100¢	$11.20	$42.00
SUGAR (RAW)* (world) #11	N.Y. Coffee & Sugar Exch. 10:00 A.M. - 3:00 P.M.	50 Tons (112,000 Lbs.)	1/100¢	$11.20	$42.00 - 5.49¢ or under $62.00 - 5.50¢ or over
WOOL* Grease/Crossbred	Wool Associates of the New York Cotton Exchange 10:00 A.M. - 2:30 P.M.	6,000 Lbs.	1/10¢	$6.00	$50.00

* Special rates for Straddles and Day Trades.   ** Special rates for Straddles.

Outside the United States, the following commodity futures are traded:

   Winnipeg: Barley, flaxseed, oats, rapeseed, and rye.

Commodities vs. Securities—What Are the Differences?

a. Margin requirements: the amount of cash someone must deposit with his broker to buy (or sell short) stocks generally ranges between 50 percent and 100 percent of the total transaction value; margin on a commodity transaction averages 10 percent—sometimes as low as 6 percent. And that's leverage!

b. Futures have maximum daily price fluctuation limits; no such limits exist in stock trading.

c. Futures contracts have a limited life, usually between 12 and 18 months, and are never paid for in full until delivery. This means that commodity traders can't put on positions and just sit with them, as investors can do with stocks. For many commodity traders, "short term" might be just a day or so, while "long term" means a few weeks or a month.

d. A commodity trader can sell short more easily than a stock trader, and is more apt to do so.

e. For any security, the total short interest is a fraction of the total long interest (total number of shares outstanding). Hence, most stock traders profit when prices advance and lose when prices decline.

It's different in commodities, where the *long and short interests are always equal,* so that the same number of long and short contracts make or lose money whichever direction the prices move.

For instance, as of February 1974, there were 145 million shares of IBM outstanding (the long interest) but only 50,000 shares short; so we can say that the short interest was less than .04 percent of the total long interest. Let's compare this with the New York silver market, where there were 65,000 contracts long *and* 65,000 contracts short.

f. Most commodities have reduced day-trade and spread (straddle) commission rates, and reduced spread margin requirements. Unfortunately, stock traders do not enjoy these reductions.

Speculators vs. Hedgers

There are two classes of commodity traders: *speculators* and trade (industry) *hedgers.*

The *speculator* trades to make *profits*—it's that simple. He is motivated by the low margin requirements and the active, broad-swinging markets. He buys if he expects a price rise and sells in expectation of a price decline, risking his own capital on his ability to forecast price movements.

The *trade hedger,* on the other hand, buys and sells futures *as part of his* marketing or merchandising *business.* He may sell futures to hedge his risk on commodities owned but not yet sold; or he may buy futures to cover delivery commitments where he doesn't yet own the required actual commodity. Examples of trade hedgers are firms such as Continental Grain, General Mills, General Cocoa, Nestle, and Engelhard Industries.

Cash vs. Futures

The cash and futures markets are separate but closely related. The *cash market* refers to the *regular commercial channels* for buying, selling, storing, and distributing actual (physical) commodities. An example would be wheat that is harvested on the farm and sold to a commercial grain-elevator operator, who may then store it for a time and perhaps sell it to a grain exporter for overseas shipment.

The *futures market* refers to the *organized exchange trading* of standardized contracts for the future delivery of commodities. The principal differences between the two markets are:

Cash transactions may take place anywhere in the world, at any time and between any parties. They are privately and usually secretly negotiated between the principals or their agents, so that the trade terms and details are likely to vary with each transaction. Examples of cash transactions are the massive grain sales to the Soviet Union which were negotiated in 1972 by a number of U.S. grain dealers.

Futures transactions may be executed only by exchange members (called floor brokers or floor traders) in the designated exchange ring or pit, during specified trading hours. All trades must be publicly announced by open outcry by the executing brokers, and a record of every transaction is noted by exchange "reporters" and disseminated to interested parties throughout the world via ticker tapes and news wires. Most of the important details of a futures contract (such as trading hours, contract specifications, margins, and commissions) are standardized, so that the only terms which vary for each transaction are the names of the buyer and seller, the delivery month, and the contract price.

Up and Down the Limit

Each exchange establishes maximum daily limits of trading, so that no trade may be executed at more than a specified number of cents above or below the previous day's settlement price—or, in some markets, above the low or below the high for that day's session. This is done to prevent violent and perhaps ruinous price fluctuations in a single trading session. It interposes an overnight "cooling-off" period which could act to moderate excessive price fluctuations, and also to give brokers a chance to issue margin calls.

For example, silver has a 20¢-per-ounce daily trading limit. Thus, if December silver closed at $5.75 (per troy ounce) on a particular day, it could not trade above $5.95, nor below $5.55 on the following day. Suppose the market on that next day was strong, and the price advanced to $5.95. If there were no sellers at $5.95 and yet there were numerous buyers at that price, the market would be "up the limit" ("limit-bid"). Shorts in that contract could be "locked in" for that day. Sometimes a market will be "limit-up" or "limit-down" several consecutive days. Great if the move is in your direction; perhaps a disaster if it is moving against you.

	Trading Unit (Contract Size)	Maximum Price Fluctuation (Advance or decline from previous close) *
Copper	25,000 pounds	5¢ per lb, or $1,250 per contract
Corn	5,000 bushels	10¢ per bu, or $ 500 per contract
Pork Bellies	36,000 pounds	1½¢ per lb, or $ 540 per contract
Silver (N.Y.)	10,000 ounces	20¢ per oz, or $2,000 per contract
Sugar (world)	112,000 pounds	1¢ per lb, or $1,120 per contract

* During periods of particularly volatile trading activity, a futures exchange may increase trading limits on its commodity futures. Examples include silver and sugar, whose trading limits were increased to 20¢ per ounce and 1¢ per pound, respectively, early in 1974.

Quotations

During the trading session, each exchange utilizes a ticker tape for each transaction listing the commodity (when the exchange lists more than one commodity), the delivery month, the price, and the time of the trade. Some exchange tickers also note the volume for each trade. In addition, many brokers' offices display computer-connected boards, or desk units, which present the same information as the ticker tape.

Many newspapers publish each day's commodity prices, as on p. 164.

The Almighty Margin

Commodity margin is technically "earnest money," a sum which the trader must deposit with his broker when he initiates a long or short position. It is a financial guarantee that the trader will fulfill his contractual obligation.

Margin requirements are set by each individual exchange as a fixed dollar amount per contract, rather than as a percentage of the total cost as in stock trading.

There are two types of margins—*initial* and *variation* (maintenance). *Initial* margin is deposited when the futures position is initiated. Subsequently, if the market moves against a position by a specified amount (usually about a 25 percent to 30 percent adverse move), the broker will call for additional margin, called *variation* (maintenance) margin, to bring the account up to full initial margin. Margin requirements are based on both the price level and the volatility of each commodity; the exchanges raise or

Futures Prices

Friday, March 8, 1974

	Open	High	Low	Close	Change	Season's High	Season's Low
CHICAGO—WHEAT							
Mar	561	562	546½	546½a	—20	645	211
May	549	549	531½	531½a	—20	636	249¼
July	517	520	497	497a	—20	585	272¾
Sept	515	519	493½	493½-494	—20to19½	582	331
Dec	514	520	495	496-497	—19to18	582	453
CORN							
Mar	309	310	299¼	299¼a	—10	343	133¼
May	315	315	304¾	304¾a	—10	349	156
July	320	320	308½	308½a	—10	353	226
Sept	314	314	303¼	303¼a	—10	345	225
Dec	292½	294	283¾	283¾a	—10	325	195
Mar75	298	298	286	286a	—10	329	214
OATS							
Mar	152	152½	140½	141	—6	178¼	100
May	157	157	145	145a	—6	185¾	102½
July	159	159	149	149a	—6	185¼	102
Sept	162	162	152½	152½a	—6	187	124
Dec	156	157	154¼	154¼a	—6	187½	153¾
SOYBEANS							
Mar	640	640	619	622	—14½	913	357
May	644	644	625	628-629	—17½to16½	906	413
July	648	649	630	632½-633	—16to15½	903	522
Aug	646	649	630	632	—17	694	519
Sept	633	635	621	621-622	—15to14	684	514
Nov	628	631¼	615	618-619	—11¾to10¾	666	510
Jan 75	633	634	619	620	—12	673	513
SOYBEAN OIL							
Mar	31.50	31.70	28.50	28.50-.80	—3.22to2.92	37.00	9.40
May	26.85	26.85	25.90	25.90a	—1.00	31.35	11.05
July	24.70	24.80	23.82	23.82a	—1.00	28.50	14.50
Aug	23.90	24.13	23.25	23.35-.25	— .78to.88	27.60	14.95
Sept	23.70	2?.90	22.85	22.85-.90	— .92to.97	26.50	14.85
Oct	22.75	22.80	22.00	22.05-22.	— .67to.72	25.20	14.70
Dec	22.20	22.40	21.40	21.60-.50	— .60to.70	24.00	14.85
Jan 75	21.40	21.40	20.50	20.50-.55	— .77to.72	23.15	19.65
SOYBEAN MEAL							
Mar	151.50	151.50	147.00	149.0-150.0	—2.5to1.5	283.00	117.00
May	158.50	159.00	155.00	157.00	—2.20	283.00	132.00
July	162.50	163.00	158.50	162.00	—1.00	284.00	152.00
Aug	163.00	163.50	160.00	162.5-163.0	— .70to.20	203.00	152.00
Sept	164.00	164.00	161.00	162.00	—1.80	178.50	156.00
Oct	166.00	166.50	162.00	164.50	—2.00	192.00	150.00
Dec	167.00	167.00	163.50	166.00b	—2.30	180.00	158.00
Jan75	168.00	168.00	165.50	167.00	—3.00	172.50	164.00
ICED BROILERS							
Mar	38.60	38.70	37.75	37.95	— .10	54.95	34.50
May	38.60	38.75	37.75	37.90	— .37	52.00	35.10
June	40.60	40.60	39.35	39.95	— .55	44.80	36.00
July	40.65	40.90	39.85	39.85-.95	— .67to.57	45.20	36.40
Aug	41.00	41.00	40.20	40.40-.50	— .55to.45	44.55	38.80
Sept	40.60	40.60	39.75	40.20	— .30	44.25	38.00
PLYWOOD							
Mar	135.00	137.00	131.00	135.00	+1.50	140.00	85.10
May	136.50	138.70	133.00	138.5-137.5	+2.8to1.8	142.50	86.50
July	137.80	139.50	135.10	138.00	+ .80	145.00	87.60
Sept	139.00	140.00	135.50	138.50	+ .50	145.00	97.00
Nov	136.50	137.00	134.00	136.00	+1.00	142.90	100.00
Jan75	136.00	136.50	132.00	134.00	+1.50	140.00	123.50
CHICAGO—SILVER							
Mar	543.00	547.00	505.00	514.00b	—33.00	641.70	480.00
Apr	543.00	543.00	509.00	520.-519.5	—3.0to3.5	641.50	205.30
May	547.00	547.00	509.00	523.00	—4.00	560.00	506.00
June	549.50	549.50	514.00	527.00-.50	—2.5to2.0	647.50	219.50
Aug	554.00	554.00	519.00	534.00-535.	unch to+1.	649.80	227.00
Oct	559.50	559.50	525.00	538.50	—1.00	651.80	273.00
Dec	562.50	562.50	528.00	542.50		653.20	275.00
Feb75	565.00	565.00	533.00	545.50	+ .50	655.00	293.00
Apr	567.50	567.50	529.00	548.50	+1.00	657.00	349.70
June	570.00	570.00	542.00	551.00	+1.00	582.00	529.50
KANSAS CITY—WHEAT							
Mar	532	536	518	518	—18	619	209½
May	540	540	513	516	—20	610	239
July	523	523	499½	503	—17	584	276
Sept	520	520	496	498	—18½	582	321
Dec	520	520	497½	501	—15	580	462
MINNEAPOLIS—WHEAT							
Mar	549	549	528	528	—17	609	244
May	540	540	514	515	—19	599	266
July	515	519	505	505	—20	589	335
Sept	517	519	494	496a	—17	581	456
WINNIPEG—RAPESEED (VANCOUVER)							
Mar	761	761	756	756	—20	817½	379¼
June	751	751	724½	724½a	—20	800	480
Sept	717	722	707	707a	—20	727	584
Nov	655	660	654	654a	—16	690	603
Jan 75	658	658	652	652a	—16	658	652
RYE							
May	359½	360	347	347	—15	403	198
July	352	352	335½	335½	—14½	387½	214½
FLAXSEED							
May	1170	1170	1130	1130	—30	1242	523
July	1135	1135	1095	1095a	—30	1192	803
Oct	1025	1025	1023	1023a	—30	1137	845
CATTLE (CHICAGO MERCANTILE EXCHANGE)							
Apr	44.95	45.15	44.17	45.15b	+1.00	62.07	40.62
June	48.00	48.20	47.10	48.20	+1.00	61.75	43.12
Aug	48.90	49.10	48.50	49.10	+1.00	60.62	42.67
Oct	49.90	50.05	49.45	50.05	+1.00	56.00	42.67
Dec	50.90	51.40	50.30	51.20-50.85	+ .73to.38	53.90	48.70
Sales estimated at: 13,091 contracts.							
FRESH EGGS							
Mar	56.25	56.25	54.50	55.15-.45	— .80to.50	72.50	43.50
Apr	54.90	54.90	53.35	54.25-.15	— .70to.80	59.60	42.00
May	52.50	52.55	51.00	51.85-.60	— .45to.70	54.30	42.00
June	52.80	52.80	51.50	52.00	— .90	54.95	44.30
July	54.50	54.50	53.90	54.15a	— .60	55.40	47.20
Aug	53.00	53.20	53.00	53.20	+ .20	55.60	52.50
Sept	58.90	59.00	58.00	58.55-.75	+ .55to.75	60.00	52.00
Oct	57.25	57.25	57.25	57.25		57.25	56.20
Sales estimated at: 1,606 contracts.							
POTATOES (IDAHO RUSSET)							
May	15.69	15.77	15.49	15.70	....	17.75	7.55
Sales: 147 contracts.							

	Open	High	Low	Close	Change	Season's High	Season's Low
FROZEN PORK BELLIES							
Mar	51.00	51.00	49.70	49.75	—1.45	82.75	45.00
May	52.00	52.00	50.72	50.72	—1.50	82.25	48.00
July	53.05	53.05	51.90	51.90	—1.50	81.10	51.10
Aug	52.80	52.80	51.22	51.22	—1.50	78.40	50.75
Feb 75	59.60	59.90	58.15	58.85a	— .80	65.80	51.60
Sales estimated at: 3,587 contracts.							
HOGS							
Apr	38.15	38.15	37.00	37.20-.10	— .95to1.05	57.60	27.15
June	40.60	40.60	39.47	39.60-.65	—1.17to1.12	58.50	35.50
July	42.80	42.85	41.75	42.-41.90	— .85to.95	57.25	35.10
Aug	43.10	43.10	41.82	42.30b	— .47	55.00	37.50
Oct	43.25	43.25	41.60	42.15-.25	— .80to.70	49.10	39.25
Dec	44.85	44.85	43.55	43.90-.70	— .95to1.15	50.45	40.10
Feb 75	46.80	46.85	45.90	45.90a	— .95	48.50	44.75
Sales estimated at: 3,875 contracts.							
LUMBER							
Mar	178.00	178.70	172.10	172.10	—4.40	178.70	108.00
May	177.00	178.80	173.00	173.00-.50	—2.4to1.9	178.80	114.00
July	174.00	176.00	170.80	171.30-.10	—1.7to1.9	176.00	117.00
Sept	170.00	172.00	165.00	166.5-166.0	—2.5to3.0	172.50	117.80
Nov	167.50	167.50	164.00	165.00b	—2.90	172.40	126.00
Sales estimated at: 1,171 contracts.							
NEW YORK—SILVER							
Mar	545.00	546.00	505.00	511.00	—34.00	643.00	193.50
Apr	521.00	521.00	514.50	514.50	—10.50	641.50	514.50
May	548.50	548.50	510.00	518.00	—10.50	644.20	208.40
July	553.60	553.60	515.00	523.80	—9.80	646.90	225.00
Sept	558.00	558.00	518.00	528.50	—9.50	649.40	231.50
Dec	563.20	563.20	525.00	534.00	—9.20	652.10	274.80
Jan75	564.50	564.50	532.00	535.50	—9.00	653.00	276.90
Mar	567.30	567.30	529.00	538.50	—8.80	655.20	291.50
May	569.60	569.60	532.00	541.20	—8.40	657.00	342.80
July	571.80	571.80	543.50	543.50	—8.30	571.80	530.90
Sales: 3,463 contracts.							
COPPER							
Mar	123.50	124.00	116.50	116.60	—4.90	140.00	55.50
May	114.60	114.80	109.00	109.60	—3.00	119.90	61.25
July	110.50	110.50	105.00	105.50	—2.70	115.50	66.50
Sept	107.00	107.00	102.00	102.50	—2.50	112.10	66.00
Oct	105.90	105.90	101.10	101.10	—2.60	110.40	67.40
Dec	103.20	104.00	98.00	98.00	—3.70	107.40	72.00
Jan75	103.00	103.00	97.90	97.90	—2.70	106.10	71.70
Mar	100.80	100.80	96.50	96.60	—2.70	104.50	79.50
Sales: 2,176 contracts.							
SUGAR (WORLD CONTRACT)							
May	19.00	20.95	18.95	19.95-.60	unch to—.35	24.46	7.05
July	17.80	19.67	17.70	18.55-.30	— .12to.37	23.25	7.05
Sept	16.30	18.12	16.12	16.25-.12	— .87to1.00	21.63	7.25
Oct	15.75	17.42	15.65	15.70-.95	— .72to.47	20.77	7.42
Mar 75	12.40	14.03	12.40	13.05-12.95	+ .02to.08	18.08	7.40
May	12.10	13.20	12.00	12.60-.95	+ .37to.72	17.45	7.80
July	11.95	12.19	11:93	12.30	+ .39	17.15	11.11
Sales: 4,532 contracts. Spot: 21.50n.							
COFFEE							
Mar	69.70	70.00	69.50	69.70b	+ .10	79.20	57.00
May	71.25	72.60	71.30	72.45-.50	— .45to.40	82.95	65.45
July	75.40	75.65	74.40	75.40-.60	— .60to.40	85.53	66.10
Sept	78.80	78.80	77.15	78.60	— .30	88.00	67.10
Nov	80.80	80.80	79.60	80.50b	— .50	89.10	69.90
Dec	79.90	80.50	79.90	80.50b	— .75	89.99	70.40
Mar 75	81.00	81.00	81.00	81.75b	no comp	81.00	81.00
Sales: 959 contracts.							
COCOA							
Mar	69.00	70.00	67.35	70.00	+1.20	73.60	31.13
May	63.95	63.95	61.12	63.75	+1.80	69.25	31.25
July	60.70	60.70	57.70	60.70	+1.70	67.65	35.90
Sept	58.60	59.30	56.20	58.80	+1.15	66.10	43.90
Dec	54.50	54.50	51.85	54.10	+ .25	58.50	43.99
Mar 75	52.00	52.00	50.80	51.25	— .10	56.00	43.25
May	50.30	50.30	48.30	49.95	— .35	54.80	43.80
July	48.75	48.75	48.70	48.70	— 4.5	48.75	47.50
Sales: 2,442 contracts.							
WOOL FUTURES							
Oct	182.0	182.5	182.0	182.5	—0.5	254.2	182.0
Dec	183.0	183.0	183.0	183.5b		248.0	183.0
Spot: 190.0n.							
ORANGE JUICE (FROZEN CONCENTRATED)							
Mar	48.45	48.50	47.75	47.80b	— .40	59.70	43.40
May	50.35	50.35	49.50	49.75	— .25	60.50	45.60
July	52.15	52.15	51.30	51.35b	— .35	60.95	44.50
Sept	53.15	53.20	52.50	52.80b	— .35	60.60	46.00
Nov	53.85	54.00	54.75	53.40b	— .30	60.00	47.50
Jan 75	54.85	54.85	54.25	54.20b	— .55	59.00	52.00
Sales estimated at: 400 contracts.							
COTTON							
May	68.60	69.80	67.70	68.70-.85	+ .55to.70	89.95	30.80
July	67.65	68.95	66.95	67.80-.95	+ .60to.75	87.40	33.20
Oct	63.20	64.10	62.05	62.75b	+ .15	77.40	39.55
Dec	60.75	61.75	59.85	60.30-.50	unch to+.20	71.10	42.25
Mar 75	60.70	61.45	59.75	60.35b	+ .10	70.20	52.25
Sales estimated at: 1,600 contracts.							
SILVER COIN FUTURES (IN DOLLARS)							
Apr	3720	3750	3540	3540	—150	4435	1434
July	3785	3834	3635	3635	—150	4500	1593
Oct	3855	3950	3705	3705	—150	4570	1731
Jan 75	3940	3943	3770	3770	—140	4630	2145
Apr	3825	3825	3825	3825	—150	4685	2200
July	4050	4050	4050	3880a	—150	4730	3288
Sales: 294 contracts.							
PLATINUM							
Apr	250.00	250.00	233.00	233.00	—10.00	293.50	142.50
July	255.00	255.00	239.00	239.00	—10.00	300.00	146.80
Oct	260.00	260.00	245.00	245.00	—10.00	306.00	153.40
Jan75	263.00	264.00	251.50	251.50	—10.00	314.50	166.00
Apr	265.00	273.00	256.00	256.00	—9.90	318.00	166.50
July	277.00	277.00	261.50	261.50	—10.00	325.50	229.50
Sales: 936 contracts.							
POTATOES (MAINE CONTRACT)							
Apr	12.30	12.40	12.00	12.00	— .15	15.40	4.26
May	15.00	15.00	14.56	14.81	+ .01	17.75	4.76
Nov	7.40	7.40	7.25	7.30	+ .05	8.60	4.40
Mar 75	9.00	9.10	8.78	8.85	no comp	9.10	8.78
Sales: 2,983 contracts.							

a-Asked. b-Bid. n-Nominal.

lower their margin requirements whenever market conditions make it advisable. Here are a few typical margin requirements as of February 1974:

Commodity	Initial Margin	Must be Maintained at
Corn	$1,500	$1,000
Cotton	6,000	4,000
Potatoes	800	500

Opening a Commodity Account

The most important part of opening a commodity account is selecting a broker. Many of the large, retail-oriented stock-exchange firms handle commodity business, as do numerous smaller commodity specialty firms. A listing of these firms can be obtained from the Commodity Exchange Authority, any of the commodity exchanges, or your bank.

Meet and talk with representatives of these firms and inquire concerning their financial condition, their commodity experience and expertise, and their physical facilities. Examine past copies of each firm's market letters and research material, and be sure that the firm's approach to research and trading is consistent with your own. For example, a technically oriented trader (a chartist) would probably not work well with a firm whose research approach was fundamentally directed.

Opening an account is quite similar to opening a securities account or a bank account. You will be asked to complete a brief form (see below), and

---

BW-105-72

BRODY, WHITE & COMPANY, INC.
TWENTY-FIVE BROAD STREET
NEW YORK, NEW YORK 10004

NEW ACCOUNT CARD

Name(s) _____
(please print)

Signature(s) _____ Date _____

Mailing Address _____ City _____ State _____ Zip _____

Telephone: Residence _____ Business _____

Type of Account   ☐ Individual   ☐ Partnership   ☐ Corporate   ☐ Joint

Is customer over 21 years of age?   ☐ Yes   ☐ No

If Power of Attorney, in favor of whom _____

Occupation _____ Name of Business _____

Bank and other reference _____

to sign a customer's agreement. This agreement has lots of small print, which I suggest you read very carefully before you sign.

The firm will generally require a margin deposit before accepting any orders, and some firms specify a minimum-size account, such as $10,000 or so. I think this is a good idea—I would discourage anyone from trading who isn't able to risk at least that amount in the market.

BACHE & CO. INCORPORATED	ACCOUNT NAME (HEREIN REFERRED TO AS I)	OFFICE	ACC. NO.	R.R.	DATE

CUSTOMER'S AGREEMENT

1. I agree as follows with respect to all of my accounts, in which I have an interest alone or with others, which I have opened or open in the future, with you for the purchase and sale of securities and commodities:

2. I am of full age and represent that I am not an employee of any exchange or of a Member Firm of any Exchange or the NASD, or of a bank, trust company, or insurance company and that I will promptly notify you if I become so employed.

3. All transactions for my account shall be subject to the constitution, rules, regulations, customs and usages, as the same may be constituted from time to time, of the exchange or market (and its clearing house, if any) where executed.

4. Any and all credit balances, securities, commodities or contracts relating thereto, and all other property of whatsoever kind belonging to me or in which I may have an interest held by you or carried for my accounts shall be subject to a general lien for the discharge of my obligations to you (including unmatured and contingent obligations) however arising and without regard to whether or not you have made advances with respect to such property and without notice to me may be carried in your general loans and all securities may be pledged, repledged, hypothecated or re-hypothecated, separately or in common with other securities or any other property, for the sum due to you thereon or for a greater sum and without retaining in your possession and control for delivery a like amount of similar securities or other property. At any time and from time to time you may, in your discretion, without notice to me, apply and/or transfer any securities, commodities, contracts relating thereto, cash or any other property therein, interchangeably between any of my accounts, whether individual or joint or from any of my accounts to any account guaranteed by me. You are specifically authorized to transfer to my cash account on the settlement day following a purchase made in that account, excess funds available in any of my other accounts, including but not limited to any free balances in any margin account or in any non-regulated commodities account, sufficient to make full payment of this cash purchase. I agree that any debit occurring in any of my accounts may be transferred by you at your option to my margin account.

5. I will maintain such margins as you may in your discretion require from time to time and will pay on demand any debit balance owing with respect to any of my accounts. Whenever in your discretion you deem it desirable for your protection, (and without the necessity of a margin call) including but not limited to an instance where a petition in bankruptcy or for the appointment of a receiver is filed by or against me, or an attachment is levied against my account, or in the event of notice of my death or incapacity, or in compliance with the orders of any Exchange, you may, without prior demand, tender, and without any notice of the time or place of sale, all of which are expressly waived, sell any or all securities, or commodities or contracts relating thereto which may be in your possession, or which you may be carrying for me, or buy any securities, or commodities or contracts relating thereto of which my account or accounts may be short, in order to close out in whole or in part any commitment in my behalf or you may place stop orders with respects to such securities or commodities and such sale or purchase may be made at your discretion on any Exchange or other market where such business is then transacted, or at public auction or private sale, with or without advertising and no demands, calls, tenders or notices which you may make or give in any one or more instances shall invalidate the aforesaid waivers on my part. You shall have the right to purchase for your own account any or all of the aforesaid property at any such sale, discharged of any right of redemption, which is hereby waived.

6. All orders for the purchase or sale of commodities for future delivery may be closed out by you as and when authorized or required by the Exchange where made. Against a "long" position in any commodity contract, prior to maturity thereof, and at least five business days before the first notice day of the delivery month, I will give instructions to liquidate, or place you in sufficient funds to take delivery; and in default thereof, or in the event such liquidating instructions cannot be executed under prevailing conditions, you may, without notice or demand, close out the contracts or take delivery and dispose of the commodity upon any terms and by any method which may be feasible. Against a "short" position in any commodity contract, prior to maturity thereof, and at least five business days before the last trading day of the delivery month, I will give you instructions to cover, or furnish you with all necessary delivery documents; and in default thereof, you may without demand or notice, cover the contracts, or if orders to buy in such contracts cannot be executed under prevailing conditions, you may procure the actual commodity and make delivery thereof upon any terms and by any method which may be feasible.

7. All transactions in any of my accounts are to be paid for or required margin deposited no later than 2:00 p.m. on the settlement date.

8. I agree to pay interest and service charges upon my accounts monthly at the prevailing rate as determined by you.

9. I agree that, in giving orders to sell, all "short" sale orders will be designated as "short" and all "long" sale orders will be designated as "long" and that the designation of a sell order as "long" is a representation on my part that I own the security and, if the security is not in your possession that it is not then possible to deliver the security to you forthwith and I will deliver it on or before the settlement date.

10. Reports of the execution of orders and statements of my account shall be conclusive if not objected to in writing within five days and ten days, respectively, after transmittal to me by mail or otherwise.

11. All communications including margin calls may be sent to me at my address given you, or at such other address as I may hereafter give you in writing, and all communications so sent, whether in writing or otherwise, shall be deemed given to me personally, whether actually received or not.

12. No waiver of any provision of this agreement shall be deemed a waiver of any other provision, nor a continuing waiver of the provision or provisions so waived.

13. I understand that no provision of this agreement can be amended or waived except in writing signed by an officer of your Company, and that this agreement shall continue in force until its termination by me is acknowledged in writing by an officer of your Company; or until written notice of termination by you shall have been mailed to me at my address last given you.

14. This contract shall be governed by the laws of the State of New York, and shall inure to the benefit of your successors and assigns, and shall be binding on the undersigned, his heirs, executors, administrators and assigns. Any controversy arising out of or relating to my account, to transactions with or for me or to this agreement or the breach thereof, shall be settled by arbitration in accordance with the rules then obtaining of either the American Arbitration Association or the Board of Governors of the New York Stock Exchange as I may elect, except that any controversy arising out of or relating to transactions in commodities or contracts relating thereto, whether executed or to be executed within or outside of the United States shall be settled by arbitration in accordance with the rules then obtaining of the Exchange (if any) where the transaction took place, if within the United States, and provided such Exchange has arbitration facilities or under the rules of the American Arbitration Association as I may elect. If I do not make such election by registered mail addressed to you at your main office within five days after demand by you that I make such election, then you may make such election. Notice preliminary to, in conjunction with, or incident to such arbitration proceeding, may be sent to me by mail and personal service is hereby waived. Judgment upon any award rendered by the arbitrators may be entered in any court having jurisdiction thereof, without notice to me.

15. If any provision hereof is or at any time should become inconsistent with any present or future law, rule or regulation of any securities or commodities exchange or of any sovereign government or a regulatory body thereof and if any of these bodies have jurisdiction over the subject matter of this agreement, said provision shall be deemed to be superseded or modified to conform to such law, rule or regulation, but in all other respects this agreement shall continue and remain in full force and effect.

DATE _____CUSTOMER'S SIGNATURE _____

A trader will find a number of brokerage statements in his mailbox from time to time. I am told that many people have trouble understanding these forms—which simply means that they never had them properly explained. Here is my explanation:

1. A *trade confirmation* (p. 168) is mailed by the broker every time a client makes a trade (buys or sells). This confirmation contains the trade

date, whether it was a purchase or sale, the commodity and the market, the number of contracts (or number of bushels of grain),* the delivery month and the price.

2. For every liquidating trade, the client receives a *purchase and sale statement* (p. 169). This statement recaps both the purchase and sale dates and prices, the gross profit or loss (before commissions), the round-turn commission, and the net profit or loss.

3. Every time an open order (good till canceled, or good through a specified date) is either entered or canceled, the broker mails out an *open-order confirmation* (p. 170). I suggest you read the fine print very carefully. It says:

As the responsibility for failure to cancel a former order when entering a substitute therefor rests upon the customer, transactions resulting from the execution of both old and new orders will be entered in the client's account.

4. Every time cash is deposited or withdrawn, the broker mails out a *debit* or *credit* memo (p. 170). You should be sure that these debit and credit entries are reflected on your . . .

5. *Monthly statement,* which is mailed by the broker as of the last business day of each month (p. 171). The monthly statement is divided into two sections:

a. The first section records the opening and closing cash balances (just as on a month-end checking-account statement), and all cash entries (such as deposits and withdrawals, and profits or losses on closed-out trades) during the entire month.

b. The second section lists the open futures positions as of the last business day of the month.

TO SUMMARIZE:

If you:	*Then you receive:*
initiate a trade (buy or sell)	a trade confirmation
close out a trade (buy or sell)	a trade confirmation, *and* a purchase and sale (P & S) statement
deposit funds	a credit memo
withdraw funds	a debit memo
enter or cancel an open order	an open order confirmation
in addition, at the end of every month	a monthly statement

* The grains—corn, wheat, oats, and soybeans—are traded in 5,000-bushel contracts.

KROLL, DALON & CO., INC,
25 BROAD STREET
NEW YORK, NEW YORK 10004

CONFIRMATION

TO   J. S. PARKER
420 EAST 80 STREET
NEW YORK, N. Y. 10021

DATE   ACCOUNT NO.
FEB 8, 1974   12425-50

NON-REGULATED

WE HAVE THIS DAY MADE THE FOLLOWING TRADES FOR YOUR ACCOUNT AND RISK

BOUGHT			SOLD		
QUANTITY	COMMODITY	PRICE	QUANTITY	COMMODITY	PRICE
			2	MAY 1974 SILVER	483.50
			3	MAY 1974 SILVER	483.60

NOTICE— It is understood and agreed that all futures transactions made by us for your account are either hedges or contemplate actual delivery and receipt of the property and payment therefor; and that all property sold for your account is sold upon the representation that you have the same in your possession actually or potentially. These transactions are made in accordance with and subject to the rules, regulations and customs of the exchange where made and also in accordance with and subject to Federal and State laws. It is understood and agreed that we reserve the right to close out transactions without notice when the margins on deposit with us (1) are exhausted, or (2) are inadequate in our judgment to protect us against price fluctuations, or (3) are below the minimum margin requirements under the rules and regulations of the exchange relating thereto.

N.B.— Any apparent error should be immediately reported by telegraph or telephone, otherwise this account will be considered approved by you. Name of other party to contract furnished on request.   E. & O.E.

*How Commodity Markets Are Regulated**

There are two categories of commodity futures: *regulated* and *unregulated*. *Regulated* commodities are those which come under the jurisdiction of the Commodity Exchange Authority (CEA), a branch of the U.S. Department of Agriculture. These are domestically produced agricultural and livestock commodities, such as corn, wheat, cattle, eggs, potatoes, and frozen orange juice. *Unregulated* commodities, those which are produced and traded internationally, such as cocoa, coffee, copper, silver, and sugar, do not come under the cognizance of the CEA. Trading in unregulated commodities is regulated by the respective futures exchanges.

In regulated commodities, the CEA functions both as a watchdog, to assure equitable rules and conduct of trading, and also as a source of information and statistics. The CEAs responsibilities include:

a. Licensing commodity exchanges (called "contract markets") which conduct trading in regulated commodities; registering brokerage firms (called "futures commission merchants") and floor brokers; establishing minimum

* Legislation is being introduced in Congress which may change the present system of commodity regulation.

STATEMENT OF ACCOUNT - PURCHASE AND SALE

J. S. PARKER
420 EAST 80 STREET
NEW YORK, N.Y. 10021

DATE
FEB 8, 1974

ACCOUNT NO
12425-50

NON-REGULATED

E.&O.E.

DATE	GRAINS IN 000'S BOUGHT	GRAINS IN 000'S SOLD	COMMODITY	TRADE PRICE	AMOUNT DEBIT	AMOUNT CREDIT
02-01-74	5		MAY 1974 SILVER	419.30		
02-08-74		2	MAY 1974 SILVER	482.50		
02-08-74		3	MAY 1974 SILVER	482.60		
			TTL GROSS PROFIT OR LOSS			31,630.00
			TTL FEES AND COMMISSIONS		227.50	
			NET PROFIT OR LOSS			31,402.50

PREPARED BY AUTOMATED COMMODITY SERVICE CORP.

RETAIN FOR TAX RECORDS

financial requirements for futures commission merchants (FCMs) and auditing their books and records.

b. Ensuring trust-fund treatment of customers' regulated margin moneys and equities by requiring FCMs to segregate and protect all such funds.

c. Establishing statutory limits on speculative market positions and trading activity, and requiring speculators who reach certain specified position limits (e.g., 200,000 bushels of corn or wheat, or 25 contracts of potatoes) to report their positions and trading activity to the CEA.

d. Preventing price manipulation, corners, and dissemination of false or misleading crop or market information; observing floor trading; and investigating and acting against alleged and apparent statutory violations.

What About Trading and Price Analysis?

1. *What are the four basic futures trading techniques?* The four speculative approaches to trading are: 1) a net long or short futures market position; 2) a net long cash (actuals) position; 3) a spread (straddle) position; and 4) trading via commodity put and call options.

Of the four, certainly the most common is the *net long or short futures*

KROLL, DALON & CO., INC.

KDC SPECIALISTS IN COMMODITY FUTURES

25 Broad Street / New York, N.Y. 10004

Date_____FEB 1, 1974_____

Dear Sir(s):

We confirm that we have ENTERED   OPEN ORDER(S) for your account as follows:

TO BUY	TO SELL
	2 MAY 1974 SILVER 483.50
	3 MAY 1974 SILVER 483.60

As the responsibility for failure to cancel a former order when entering a substitute therefor rests upon the customer, transactions resulting from the execution of both old and new orders will be entered in the client's account.

KROLL, DALON & CO., INC.
25 BROAD STREET
NEW YORK, NEW YORK 10004

STATEMENT OF ACCOUNT - PURCHASE AND SALE

J. S. PARKER
420 EAST 80 STREET
NEW YORK, N. Y. 10021

DATE   ACCOUNT NO

FEB 21, 1974   12425-50

E.&O.E.

DATE	GRAINS IN 000'S BOUGHT	SOLD	COMMODITY	TRADE PRICE	AMOUNT DEBIT	CREDIT
			BEGINNING LEDGER BALANCE			62,690.75
02-21-74			CHECK DISBURSED		15,000.00	
			NEW LEDGER BALANCE			47,690.75

PREPARED BY AUTOMATED COMMODITY SERVICE CORP.   RETAIN FOR TAX RECORDS

KROLL, DALON & CO., INC.
25 BROAD STREET
NEW YORK, NEW YORK 10004

STATEMENT OF ACCOUNT - OPEN TRADES

J. S. PARKER
420 EAST 80 STREET
NEW YORK, N. Y. 10021

DATE

FEB 28, 1974

ACCOUNT NO.

12425-50

NON-REGULATED

E.&O.E.

* GRAINS IN 000's

DATE	POSITION * LONG	POSITION * SHORT	COMMODITY	TRADE PRICE	SETTLEMENT PRICE	OPEN TRADE EQUITY DEBIT	OPEN TRADE EQUITY CREDIT
02-01-74			BEGINNING LEDGER BALANCE				34,350.00
02-04-74			P & S 5 MAR SILVER				
02-07-74			P & S 1 NOV COFFEE				535.00
02-08-74			P & S 5 MAY SILVER				548.75
02-14-74			P & S 1 SEP SILVER			2,145.50	31,402.50
02-19-74			CHECK DISBURSED			2,000.00	
02-21-74			CHECK DISBURSED			15,000.00	
			ENDING LEDGER BALANCE				47,690.75
			OPEN POSITION				
11-26-73	5		MAY 1974 COCOA	46.95			
11-28-73		5	JULY 1974 COCOA	47.52			
01-17-74		4	APR 1974 PLATINUM	175.40			
01-17-74		4	OCT 1974 PLATINUM	183.60			
12-17-73	3		SEP 1974 SILVER	318.80			
12-18-73	3		SEP 1974 SILVER	327.20			
01-17-74	2		DEC 1974 SILVER	382.30			

DATA PROCESSING BY AUTOMATED COMMODITY SERVICE CORP.

RETAIN FOR TAX RECORDS

position. A speculator who is bullish on a commodity will buy, probably, a four-month to twelve-month future; if he is bearish he will sell (short), probably, a four-month to twelve-month future. If the trader proves right on the market and in the timing of his trade, he can probably make more money on a minimum investment than in any other trading or investment area.

Straddle (spread) *trading* involves the simultaneous purchase and sale of two like or related futures. Examples: long July silver vs. short December silver; long September copper in New York vs. short an equivalent copper position in London; long Chicago wheat vs. short Kansas City wheat. The straddle trader is not primarily concerned with whether prices move up or down; rather, he is interested in the price difference between his long and short "legs." He wants his long leg to advance in price *relative to* his short leg—that's how he makes his money. Straddle trading is more technical and complicated than outright long or short trading, involves smaller margins, and if done properly, involves less risk than outright trading.

"Hey, buddy, where should we deliver your potatoes?" Although most traders live in mortal fear of getting delivery, many experienced operators use the *actuals* (cash) *market* as an adjunct to their futures trading. Remember, the long-position trader will ultimately receive delivery if he has not sold out his position prior to the delivery month. In those markets where the commodities are easily storable and redeliverable, such as silver and platinum, there may be advantages to taking delivery and maintaining one's long position in actuals rather than in futures. And it's easy to close out the actuals position; just sell (short) the nearest future and instruct your broker to make delivery of your actuals against the short position. Then someone else can worry about "where to put all the potatoes."

Commodity put and call options, traded in unregulated commodity futures in both New York and London, provide a fine opportunity for limited-risk speculation in fast-moving, volatile commodity markets. This can be particularly interesting, because those free-swinging markets which offer the greatest profit potential usually involve the greatest risks. A *call option* gives the holder the right to "call," or buy, a specified quantity of the commodity future at a price specified in the option contract, on or before a specified date. A *put option* gives the holder the right to "put" or sell a specified quantity of the commodity future at a price specified in the option contract, on or before a specified date. A double option is a combination put and call on the same commodity; but only one side, either the put or the call, may be exercised. Commodity options are usually available for periods of three to fourteen months, with the cost (the premium) increasing with the life of the option.

2. *What are the two approaches to commodity price analysis?* The *fundamental approach* is based on an analysis of the economic factors underlying the commodity. It seeks to determine the basic causes of price change, as rooted primarily in supply-demand relationships. It asks the primary question: What should the price be under the given economic conditions?

The *technical approach,* on the other hand, is concerned with the behavior of the market, as expressed by the price, trading volume, and open interest. The technician relies on the daily and longer-term action of the market, via the ticker tape and the price charts, to help him determine when to buy, to sell, or to stand aside.

3. *What does "open interest" mean?* Open interest designates the total number of contracts open for a given commodity. The size of the open long position, by definition, equals the size of the open short position. For example, in February 1974 the open interest in New York silver was 65,000 contracts—meaning 65,000 long contracts *and* 65,000 short contracts. This is very different from the stock market, where the short position for a given stock is just a fraction of the total long position.

4. *What are "support" and "resistance"?* I would define a *support area* as that price level at which sufficient buying enters, or is expected to enter,

the market, to prevent further price declines, and from which level prices can rally (see chart below). A *resistance area* would be that price level at which sufficient selling enters, or is expected to enter, the market, to prevent further price advance, and from which level prices can decline. The technical analyst believes that once a support level has been penetrated by a declining market, that level then turns into an (overhead) resistance level; once a resistance level has been penetrated by an advancing market, that level then turns into a support level (see chart below). My own experience supports this thesis.

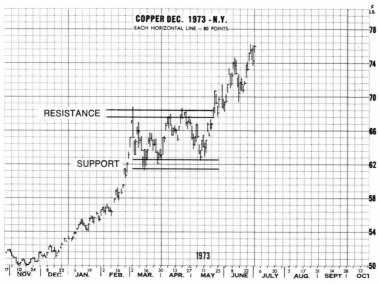

Commodity Chart Service, Commodity Research Bureau Inc.

Index